ENGLISH COUNTRY HOUSE INTERIORS

JEREMY MUSSON
Foreword by Sir Roy Strong

PHOTOGRAPHY BY PAUL BARKER
Additional photographs from Country Life

ENGLISH COUNTRY HOUSE INTERIORS

RIZZOLI
NEW YORK

New York · Paris · London · Milan

To my friend, John Hardy, for sharing
his infectious enthusiasm for the country
house interior with me and so many others,
over many years. JM

First published in the United States of America in 2011
by Rizzoli International Publications, Inc.
300 Park Avenue South, New York, NY 10010

www.rizzoliusa.com

2011 2012 2013 / 10 9 8 7 6 5 4 3 2 1

Designed and typeset in Verdigris by Dalrymple
Printed in China

ISBN: 978-0-8478-3569-0

Library of Congress Cataloging-in-Publication Data
Musson, Jeremy.
English country house interiors / Jeremy Musson ;
foreword by Roy Strong ; photography by Paul Barker ;
additional photography by Country life.
   p. cm.
Includes bibliographical references and index.
ISBN: 978-0-8478-3569-0
I. Interior decoration—England. 2. Country homes–
England. 1. Country life (London, England) II. Title.
NK2043.M87 2011
748'.880942–dc22

                              2011010426

Endpapers: Carlyle Damask, ca. 1828,
Hamilton Weston Wallpapers

Frontispiece: A detail of the early-eighteenth-century
chair from Richmond House in the music room at
Goodwood House, Sussex

Foreword

ENGLISH COUNTRY HOUSE INTERIORS REMAIN ONE OF THE WONDERS of the civilized world. Thanks to the law of primogeniture, a house and its contents would descend intact in the male line, unless disaster struck. The choice of focussing in this book on the interiors alone reflects something that sets English houses apart. They are never showy on the outside. Exteriors are always concerned with sobriety and silhouette, which only heightens the revelation when the door is thrown open and the visitor enters to be astonished by the dazzling opulence within. But even inside there is a hierarchy, for what we see here are the state rooms and rooms of parade or display that were never used except on the grandest of occasions, those occupied by the family being far smaller in scale and more muted in decoration. Such houses in previous centuries were, of course, meant to impress but also were designed to be cultural oases where it was possible to see Old Master paintings, antique sculpture, assemblies of rarities, and substantial libraries, as well as collections of drawings, engravings, and manuscripts. What also sets them apart is again uniquely English, for as the country was governed by a ruler subject to the rule of Parliament, the country house was no mere retreat from the court but the owner's power base. Through his estate he was able to control who was elected to Parliament and other officers within the locality. The existence of state rooms for the monarch reflected that it was the ruler who came to the owner and not the other way around. Finally, and again unlike on the mainland, owners were buried in their local parish church, which they treated as their dynastic chapel.

What the reader will find more surprising is the continued vitality of the English country house. The inclusion of houses like Parham and Berkeley Castle as epitomising a new stylistic phase in the twentieth century is refreshing and original. After the cataclysm of the final collapse of aristocratic power, the disappearance of servants, and the punitive taxation after 1945, all of which took a terrible toll in terms of lost houses, the position stabilized. Virtually all of the houses here are lived in still by families who have made the adjustment to opening to the public and also responded to the huge advances in our knowledge about such interiors, often by putting them back as they were when conceived. In addition, there is an increasing desire to celebrate the present. Moreover, this elegant and thoughtful book brings the eye of a new generation to the interiors of these important houses, and will engage the interest of a wide new audience to their great significance.

Sir Roy Strong

Designed by Vanbrugh for the 3rd Earl, the vaulted corridors at Castle Howard in Yorkshire were the perfect repository for the sculpture collection of the 4th Earl.

English Country House Interiors

THE ENGLISH COUNTRY HOUSE IS NOW A ROMANTIC IDEAL, BUT historically it was a pragmatic institution. The prime residence of a land-owning family, the country house was supported and sustained by the land around it. Land meant status, position, and a place in the legislature, as peers or MPs. The architecture of the country house thus spoke of power and civilisation; its interiors were a social paradigm into which the greatest skills in decorating and furnishing were poured.[1]

Country house interiors were the setting for every aspect of life for a noble family. To this end, interiors reflected the styles of royal palaces, producing magnificent, memorable, and rare examples of taste, discernment, and wealth, which survive to amaze and puzzle the modern gaze. This book gives an account of some fourteen of the grandest country house interiors—most still the homes of the families for whom, and by whom, they were built. These houses contain collections of paintings, sculpture, and furnishings that could compete with major museums and galleries; indeed the first public museums and galleries were conceived as reflections of just such interiors. Country houses of the leading aristocracy were intended to promote the national interest, the arts, and manufacture, and some were intended as symbolic temples to the muses. Beauty and magnificence were a national duty.

The houses selected are the historic seats of great landowners; today they are all opened to and enjoyed by a wide public. But they also remain what they were designed to be: homes. These houses are not museum sets, and most have been the subject of processes of restoration and redisplay for the pleasure of the visiting public as much as for the families who own them. This account looks at how what survives informs our understanding of different periods: from Jacobean, to the Baroque, the Palladian, the neoclassical, and the stylistic choices of the nineteenth century (neoclassical, Gothic Revival, and Louis XIV), to the restorations of the interwar period, in part inspired by Arts and Crafts and Aesthetic movement values.

Interior decoration has a history as long as architecture. Where there are buildings, there will be decoration—especially when status needs to be expressed. We know from excavations in Rome and Pompeii that grand interiors of the ancient world were full of colour, detail, and richness, with walls painted with mythological subjects and trompe l'oeil architecture, mosaic floors, and carved and gilded furniture. This would also have been true of the villas of Roman Britain.[2]

England's grand interiors before and up to the early medieval period are only hinted at through surviving elements of wall decoration and features such as carved ceilings. However, they are evoked by the vividly coloured pictures in illuminated manuscripts. The archaeologically inclined aesthetic of the early

Comfort and display: the entrance hall at Kelmarsh Hall, Northamptonshire, photographed in 1933, as decorated by Nancy Lancaster (with advice from Mrs. Guy Bethell), combining that sense of everyday living and comfort in what is to modern eyes almost impossible grandeur.

twentieth century tended to strip down such interiors to enjoy them as slightly melancholic shells of stone. But this subdued aesthetic was an invention. In reality, walls were covered in colourful hangings or painted decoration. From the thirteenth century, floors often featured bright tile designs, and colour was the vibrant setting for much social and religious ritual.

In the medieval houses of the nobility, tapestry, usually imported from France and the Low Countries, gave full-length depictions of gardens, figurative subjects, biblical stories, or hunting scenes. Prestige items of furniture included the principal beds, made up in costly materials, canopied, and curtained, but given the peripatetic nature of medieval nobility, there was little standing furniture that could not be packed away with ease. The Great Hall held benches and tables formed of boards on trestles, and perhaps a cupboard of shelves to display silver and gilt plate.[3]

The late-sixteenth-century plasterwork ceiling and ornate carved chimneypiece at South Wraxall Manor, Wiltshire

Elizabethan grandeur: the ornate plasterwork frieze in the 1590s High Great Chamber at Hardwick Hall, Derbyshire

Timber screens used to create a concealing entrance provided a surface for elaborate carving or painting. Timber wainscot or panelling, admired for its durability and insulation, became a common feature from the end of the thirteenth century and continued into the sixteenth century, when handsomely carved linen-fold panelling was a widely used visual gesture to the tradition of textile wall hangings.

By the Tudor period, new ideas about design emanated from Renaissance Italy and France. Classical models were absorbed through the then-novel medium of printed books and the activities of itinerant French and Flemish craftsmen.[4] Chimneypieces, doorways, and other details were copied from engravings, which popularised grotesque and strapwork designs. (Strapwork is a mannerist pattern that gives the impression that it has been cut from a thick material; grotesque work was derived from wall paintings in excavated ancient Roman houses—grotesque from *grotta*, Italian for cave, as the excavated houses resemble caves.) From the mid-sixteenth century, improved manufacturing techniques of glass making, first in Italy and then in France,

Flanders, and then England itself, led to windows made from hundreds of small glass pieces. Already a status symbol because of the high cost, windows also allowed for stained-glass displays of heraldry.

Plasterwork ceilings were widely employed from the late fifteenth century for both their decorative and insulating qualities. Plasterers drew on the same pictorial sources as painted and carved decoration, incorporating classical references and family armorials.[5] Imported woven carpets were used to cover tables; textile curtains were found on beds rather than windows. Embroidered floor cushions were common in grand interiors until upholstered chairs become a feature in the early seventeenth century, when tapestry workshops were founded in England at Mortlake.

Inigo Jones's classicizing approach to architecture and interiors, informed by his travels to Italy in 1596 and 1613–14, was hugely influential throughout

Flooded with light: a bay window in the mid-sixteenth century Long Gallery at Haddon Hall, Derbyshire

From print to plaster: a detail of the early-seventeenth-century ceiling in the Long Gallery (now library) at Blickling Hall, Norfolk, featuring an emblem from Henry Peacham's Minerva Britannia *(1612)*

the seventeenth century. He incorporated external architectural details, such as the pedimented doorcase, but also admired the richness of Italian mannerist interiors, which he felt fitted the decorum of palaces of royalty and nobility: while gravity was expected outside, there should be the opportunity to entertain and dazzle within. Jones was admired for reviving true Roman interiors and ranked alongside Palladio, who had revived true Roman exterior architecture.[6]

Jones's influence continued in the work of his assistant, John Webb, and others. In the years after the Restoration in 1660, the richness of interior decoration was delivered through ornate plasterwork and carved panelling, with naturalistic motifs and allusions to classical gods and goddesses.

France remained an important source of inspiration. Visiting Paris in 1665, Sir Christopher Wren brought back engravings "that I might give our Country-Men Examples of Ornaments and Grotesks."[7] He observed a thousand men at work on the palace of the Louvre, and his own rigorous organisation at the Office of Kings Works encouraged a school of skilled craftsmen.

Plasterers such as Goudge, Grove and Martin worked in the major country houses, and plasterwork and woodcarving reached a new pitch of expressiveness, exemplified by the ceilings and staircase balusters of Sudbury Hall in Derbyshire and Belton House in Lincolnshire.

Restoration-era panelling incorporated a smooth bolection moulding (a rare English Baroque innovation) into panelled schemes, which lasted until the Palladian revival of the 1720s. Designers also favoured a restrained bolection-moulded marble chimneypiece, while furniture upholstered in costly materials added to the colour and drama of interiors.

Baroque-style proper appeared in houses whose owners were inspired by Versailles, the most admired palace of Europe. Louis XIV was responsible for a taste for gilded, silver, and jewelled furniture, and the use of mirrors—theatre being the essence of the Baroque style. His chief designer responsible for these

The magnificent carved baluster of the 1670s great staircase at Sudbury Hall, Derbyshire

An ornate, compartmented ceiling at Belton House, Lincolnshire, typical of decorative plasterwork of the 1660s and 1670s

interiors and their furnishings was Charles Le Brun. The Baroque was really launched in England by the palatial grandeur of Hugh May's work at Windsor Castle during the 1670s. Its spread was encouraged, ironically, by the revocation of the Edict of Nantes in 1685, which outlawed the Protestant church in France and meant that many French Huguenot craftsmen came to England.[8]

Metalworker Jean Tijou worked at Hampton Court and Chatsworth; many of those who worked on Boughton were Huguenots. There were ceilings and mural painting by French painters such as Laguerre or Cheron. The furniture of Andre-Charles Boulle, combining marquetry and ormolu, was also highly prized. The Baroque style was led by architects including William Talman and Sir John Vanbrugh, who used Italian mural painters, such as Antonio Verrio at Burghley House and Pellegrini at Kimbolton Castle.

In the late seventeenth century, there was an explosion of interest in oriental designs as the East India Company brought in carpets and painted and printed cottons, lacquer, tortoiseshell, and porcelain. These were commonly called "Indian," being shipped by East India merchants. Daniel Defoe referred

The theatre of the English Baroque: the all-encompassing splendour of the 1690s Heaven Room, at Burghley House, Lincolnshire, painted by Antonio Verrio

to the influence of Queen Mary's "love of fine East India calicoes" influencing taste for imports, which distressed English textile workers.[9]

From around 1690, William III brought over Flemish and French craftsmen, including Daniel Marot, who had collaborated closely with Jean Bérain, the principal designer to Louis XIV. At Hampton Court in the early 1690s, Marot designed everything from chimneypieces to the upholstered armchairs.[10] His elaborate designs for canopies of thrones and state beds were particularly influential, and he published more than one hundred engravings. England became increasingly captivated by the French taste for rich, harmonious interiors. Window curtains appeared, especially pull-up or festoon curtains, with tall mirrors between windows reflecting candlelight. High-backed chairs had seats caned or upholstered in damask or velvet.

The revival of the classical Palladian style (dominant in the 1720–40s) is associated with Lord Burlington and the 1st Earl of Leicester. It was rooted in their travels in Italy on the Grand Tour, their observation of classical remains, and their admiration for *I Quattro Libri* of late-sixteenth-century architect Andrea Palladio, designer of the country villas of the Venetian aristocracy. The Palladian style was pursued by both architects and nobleman with surprising intensity; it was dubbed "The Rule of Taste."[11] The architect Colen Campbell was a key Palladian champion whose *Vitruvius Britannicus* included such recent buildings as Wilbury House in Wiltshire and Wanstead House in Essex, alongside the houses by Inigo Jones and John Webb. It was a work of design propaganda that openly attacked the "affected and licentious" Baroque designs of Bernini and Fontana.[12] While architects pursued the pure classical ideal of Palladio in architecture, their interiors—following Jones's dictum— were richly appointed with elaborate Baroque furniture, seats, side tables, mirrors, picture frames, and chimneypieces. Describing the glorious interiors of Houghton in 1756, Mrs. Lybbe Powys wrote, "the fitting up of the furniture very superb; and the cornishes and mouldings of all apartments being gilt, it makes the whole what I call magnificently glaring."[13]

The designer William Kent (a protégé of Burlington who had studied painting in Rome) provided entire room schemes with furniture carved and gilded, drawing on Baroque models. Rooms were often dominated by two-tiered chimneypieces modelled on those of Inigo Jones and Webb, themselves sourced from the engravings of Jean Barbet. Interiors were generally given a noticeably architectural character, with doorcases that had pediments and frames. Elaborate plasterwork displaced the large-scale ceiling and wall paintings seen at Burghley. Plasterwork in stucco (plaster mixed with marble dust) was carried out by itinerant Italian stuccadores from Ticino: Bagutti, Artari, Serena, Cortese, and Vassalli.[14] This incorporated lively relief decoration often with the same figures and scenes drawn from classical mythology that had appeared in mural paintings.

With the rise of Palladian taste came a passion for collecting paintings and classical sculptures. English aristocrats who had made the Grand Tour inspected the best art collections in Rome, Venice, Florence, and Naples, and the role of display in underlining connoisseurship became a defining characteristic. Rooms dedicated to artwork acquired while travelling are a standard feature of the eighteenth-century country house.[15]

In the early eighteenth century, the lighter Rococo style arrived from France. While largely overlooked by architects, it was important in furniture design and resulted in delicate, lively plasterwork and design. The Rococo style influenced textiles and wallpaper—the famous *toiles de jouy* being a typical example. Wallpapers become more popular from the 1740s—the era of print rooms decorated by engravings pasted to walls in paper frames. Rococo also led to an interest in imported hand-painted Chinese wallpaper, furniture, and plasterwork (as seen in the Chinese Room at Claydon in Buckinghamshire), and Gothic decoration, as championed by Strawberry Hill's Horace Walpole, who saw it as a national style.[16]

This was also the age of the cabinetmaker. The best known (as a result of his masterly published pattern books) was Thomas Chippendale. His *The Gentleman and Cabinet-Maker's Director* (1754) is full of clues to the mid-century approach to decoration; he refers to a bed "with carved Cornices which may be gilt, or covered with the same stuff as the Curtains," to "A China-Case, very

proper for a Lady's Dressing-Room. It may be made of any soft Wood, and japanned any Colour." Elsewhere he says that chairs "are usually covered with the same Stuff as the Window-Curtains."[17]

The architecture and decoration of the ancient world continued to provide critical inspiration for interiors, rekindled anew by excavations at Herculaneum and Pompeii from the 1740s. This new neoclassical style, delicate and highly decorative, was championed by architects Sir William Chambers and Robert and James Adam. Horace Walpole called interiors in this style "all gingerbread, filigraine and fan-painting,"[18] but Adam, who had visited Pompeii himself, wrote in his *Works in Architecture* that "Greater variety of form, greater beauty in design, greater gaiety and elegance of ornament, are introduced into interior decoration" in his own work. Of the Palladian style he had displaced, he said, "The massive entablature, the ponderous compartment ceiling, the tabernacle frame, almost the only species of ornament formerly known, in this country, are now universally exploded."[19]

The ornamental intricacy of the plasterwork was paired with painted panels,

From left to right

A detail of the exotic 1760s decoration in the Chinese Room at Claydon House, Buckinghamshire, with carving by Luke Lightfoot

The Whistlejacket Room at Wentworth Woodhouse, Yorkshire, decorated in 1745–50 by Palladian architect Henry Flitcroft

A late-1750s Rococo chimneypiece in the Gothick Room at Temple Newsam, Yorkshire

*Gothic grandeur:
the 1750s Gothic revival
library at Arbury Hall,
Warwickshire, designed by
Sir Roger Newdigate*

*Neoclassical grandeur:
the 1760s dining room at
Kedleston Hall, Derbyshire,
photographed in 1913*

and Adam often designed the floors with carpets supplied by Axminster or Moorfields to reflect the patterns and colours of the ceilings. Damask was still much used, and Adam designed several rooms around Gobelins tapestries.

In the Regency era, the Romantic movement and the Picturesque informed a new vision of nature, and there was, at the same time, an expectation of comfort, rather than formal elegance inside the house. In *Collected Fragments* (1816), Humphry Repton summed up the change: "the most recent modern custom is, to use the library as the general living room; and that sort of state room, formerly called the best parlour, and, of late years, the drawing room, is now generally found a melancholy apartment, when entirely shut up, and only opened to give visitors a formal cold reception."[20] Repton had the solution: "but," he writes, "if such a room opens into an adjoining one, and the two are fitted up with the same carpet, curtains etc., they then become, in some degree,

Regency richness: the 1820s Louis XVII-style Elizabeth Saloon at Belvoir Castle, Rutland

one room; and the comfort of that which has books, or musical instruments, is extended in its space to that which has only sofas, chairs and card tables." In the early 1800s myriad styles were available to the patron, from the neoclassical to Gothic revival and chinoiserie. The Prince Regent was a considerable patron of architects, decorators, and cabinetmakers, and commissioned not only classical interiors filled with French or French-style furniture but also the chinoiserie Brighton Pavilion. Thomas Hope was a leading English champion of the more austere Greek revival style. In some houses during the early nineteenth century, such as Belvoir Castle, different styles were used for different rooms.[21]

In the early nineteenth century, the Gothic style became even more popular, encouraged by the geographical isolation of Britain during the Napoleonic Wars. While neo-Elizabethan and Jacobean styles were used throughout the 1840s and 1850s, medieval-inspired Gothic revival was considered appropriate for new houses on historic estates as a way of stressing the antiquity of the family.[22] A.W.N. Pugin promoted Gothic as especially English and

Regency monumental: the dining room at Belvoir Castle, designed in 1817

Christian. Charles Eastlake's *Hints on Household Taste in Furniture, Upholstery and Other Details* championed the Gothic, with attacks on the early Victorian taste for "Louis" furniture and decoration. Heraldic artists such as Thomas Willement supplied wallpapers and stained glass. Key firms of decorators included Gillows of Lancaster and Crace of London. Arts and Crafts pioneer William Morris founded his famous firm in 1862 and had considerable influence on English taste; interior decoration along Arts and Crafts principles can be seen at Standen in Sussex and Wightwick Manor, near Wolverhampton. Edwin Lutyens's designs exemplify a version of that aesthetic, from the simple, traditional interiors of Munstead Wood to Castle Drogo in Devon.[23]

From the beginning of the nineteenth century there was an interest in collecting antiques, rather than commissioning new pieces. The Treasurer's House in York, restored from the 1890s onwards by industrialist Frank Green,

Aesthetic touches: the Great Parlour at Wightwick Manor, Staffordshire, completed in 1893 to a decorative scheme by C. E. Kempe including Morris and Co. papers and textiles

The romance of the past: the 1860s Gothic revival Great Hall at Thoresby Hall, Nottinghamshire, designed by Anthony Salvin

shows how private collectors used antiques from different periods to create the equivalent of period room interiors. An interest in eighteenth-century French style is also reflected in interiors such as Waddesdon Manor and Cliveden, where rooms were fitted with carved and often painted panelling acquired directly from the houses for which they had been designed in Paris and elsewhere.[24]

In the early twentieth century, the powerful attractions of ancient domestic architecture were at their height. From 1903 William Waldorf Astor carried out an extensive restoration of Hever Castle in Kent, while Lady Baillie pursued a similar project at Leeds Castle. In the 1920s, the 8th Earl of Berkeley restored his family seat at Berkeley Castle. In all these cases, antique furniture and fittings were brought in to return the houses to a part-authentic, part-aesthetic vision of their historic beauty. Modernism did not have a major impact on the world of the grander country house,[25] although in the 1920s Samuel Courtauld commissioned startlingly new interiors at Eltham Palace, alongside his restoration of the Tudor Great Hall. Mostly, in the world of the great country houses, there was a growing sense of conservative and romantic nostalgia, although this was undoubtedly touched by North American standards of comfort, heating, and plumbing.

The middle of the twentieth century was a difficult time for the English country house. High taxation and economic depression in the late 1920s and '30s, and the upheavals of the Second World War, almost brought an end to the cultural ensemble of the country house. Country houses were sold, collections and furnishings dispersed by auctions, and many houses of considerable importance demolished.[26] A number of houses passed into the ownership of the National Trust, which has played an important role, along with the Victoria and Albert Museum, in championing interest in the country house to a wider audience. In 1973 the Historic Houses Association was also formed to promote the interests of the privately owned country house and has

The art deco entrance hall of Eltham Palace, Middlesex, designed by Rolf Engstromer for Samuel Courtauld in 1937 in a daringly modern spirit for a house attached to a restored Tudor Great Hall

The inspiration of the Arts and Crafts movement: the 1890s Oak Gallery at Munstead Wood, Surrey, designed by Edwin Luytens

played an important role ever since. Public access and international tourism have underlined the continuing national and cultural importance of the great English country houses.

The years after the Second World War were a period of austerity; interior decoration was effectively sidelined by lack of funds and materials. The worn and fading grandeur of the great country houses became almost a style in itself, a celebration of a nonchalant disdain for novelty that was out of key with the long tradition of expenditure. The professional interior decorator had become an established figure of the country house world in the interwar years, and those who linked the world of the 1930s to that of the 1950s include Felix Harbord, Ronald Fleming, John Fowler, Sibyl Colefax, and Nancy Lancaster.[27]

The change in taste and attitude with regard to the interiors of the historic house in the later twentieth century and early twenty-first (with the continuing debate over "authenticity versus taste") is discussed at the end of this book. Suffice it to say, the great challenge to owners of historic houses, curators, advisers, and decorators is to find a balance between the same key strands of comfort and display that have always been at the centre of this story.

1 HATFIELD HOUSE

The Courtly Jacobean Interior

HATFIELD HOUSE IN HERTFORDSHIRE IS ONE OF THE GREATEST surviving courtier houses of the early seventeenth century. The estate of Hatfield, along with an older house—a former bishop's palace that had become a royal property—was given to the Cecil family by King James I. This was in exchange for their famous house at Theobalds in 1607. So a new house was built at Hatfield for Robert Cecil, 1st Earl of Salisbury (1563–1612), the son of Queen Elizabeth's faithful Lord High Treasurer and himself the hard-working principal civil servant of James I and a statesman of great influence.[1]

For the poetical entertainment when Theobalds was formally presented to

A detail of strapwork ornament carved by John Bucke on the oak screen in the Marble Hall at Hatfield House, Hertfordshire

the queen, Ben Jonson wrote a performance in which the genius of the house refers to how Salisbury "now in the twilight of sere age, /Begin to seek a habitation new; /and all his fortunes, and himself, engage, /unto a seat his fathers never knew." The instructions for the stage set of this performance included a "glorious place ... erected with columns and architrave, frieze and cornice, in which were placed diaphanal glasses, filled with several waters that shewed like so many stones of orient and transparent hues." The visual ambition of these masques and entertainments was equally projected in the interiors of great houses in the novelty and profusion of ornament.[2]

So at Hatfield, as in all Renaissance-inspired interiors of the great Jacobean houses, we should imagine ourselves moving through a world of carefully planned spaces. These spaces were filled with not just the permanent carving and decorated architectural elements that survive, but rich textiles, Oriental carpets, extravagant and colourful dress, and servants in attendance in rich livery. Everywhere a sense of excitement in novelty, or "curiosity" was made manifest. Salisbury, who had grown up amongst the grandest interiors of the day, travelled to France on diplomatic missions and knew the much-admired palace at Fontainebleau. He was considered a connoisseur.

When Salisbury began to build a huge new house "of better fame" at Hatfield in 1607, Robert Lyminge was his principal surveyor or architect—and he enjoyed additional advice from Inigo Jones and from Simon Basil, the Surveyor of the Royal Works.[3] Architecture and rich interiors were hard-working Salisbury's great extravagance, for he had also built a new mansion on the Strand, a London palace completed by 1602, and commissioned the nearby New Exchange, as well as works to Cranborne Manor in Dorset. His financial adviser John Daccombe at one point in 1611 wrote to him, "I beseech your Lordship to forbear buildings."[4]

When Salisbury first visited Hatfield he wrote that he went "to view upon what part of ground I should place my new habitation where I doubt not ere long to have the honor to see my great Master"[5]; therefore, we know he conceived of his house from the start as one capable of receiving his master the king

The south front of Hatfield House, begun in 1607, with the classical loggia designed by Inigo Jones. The Long Gallery runs along the first floor.

A detail of the richly carved stonework around the south entrance of Hatfield House, including armorial decoration and strapwork ornament

and senior members of the court together, so hospitality on a grand scale was key to these interiors. The core of the new house, which was planned in every way to celebrate his own dignity and to reflect glory on his royal master, was a great suite of highly decorated state rooms in which Salisbury could fittingly entertain his monarch, with a private family apartment on the ground floor and separate lavish apartments on the first floor for both the king and queen.

From what survives and from descriptions in inventories and bills, we can tell that the interior decoration was extravagant in cost and considered original in effect. Much of the ornament was a type drawn from Italian Renaissance architectural treatises and decorative grotesque work. Grotesque work was inspired by the work of Raphael and others in the decoration of the loggia of the Vatican and sourced in excavations of ancient Roman houses such as Nero's Golden House (the word *grotesque* comes from the Italian word *grotta* for an underground cave). These decorative exemplars were circulated around Europe through French and Flemish engravings.

At Hatfield the decorative work to the interior was carried out by an impressive cast of English, French, and Flemish craftsmen—Henry Peacham's *The Art of Drawing* especially praised Salisbury's employment of "excellent Artistes for the beautifying of his house."[6] The plasterwork at Hatfield was mostly by James Leigh and carving by John Bucke, with joinery by Samuel Jenever, although Flemish and French artists were also employed. The decorative painter Rowland Buckett was especially well travelled, having accompanied ambassadors bearing gifts to Sultan Mehemmet III and his mother in Turkey.

Richard Symons noted that Buckett was "the only man that doth understand

Looking through the decorative screens passage through to the Great Hall, known as the Marble Hall

perspective [modern Italian style] of all the painters in London."7 This would have been a great claim at a time when the skills of Italian Renaissance painters were preeminent throughout Europe and touched every aspect of decoration as well as painting. The pace of works at Hatfield must have been rushed, for when the king dined with Salisbury at Hatfield in July 1611, the architecture and decoration would have been largely complete. Salisbury died in 1612.

The house was originally entered through an open arcade on the south side (the arches were later filled with a screen in 1834), illustrating the new emphasis on symmetry in architecture. This created an elegant entrance, inspired by Italian Renaissance examples probably suggested by Inigo Jones, which set the tone for the glorious rooms that followed. Enough survives today, despite the intervention of different generations, to suggest how vibrantly alive the principal rooms looked four hundred years ago, ablaze with gilding and bright colours.

The vast Great Hall, now known as the Marble Hall, with its ornate roof, was always the most visually exciting of the interiors, rising through two storeys of the house and of a scale to awe the grandest visitor. Capable of accommodating everything from large ceremonial meals to theatrical performances, the space retains much of its original oak wainscot panelling and ornamental plasterwork, although the wall decoration and painted panels within the plasterwork ribs of the Jacobean ceiling were painted by the Italian artist Taldini in 1878. The ceiling paintings replaced the original roundel depictions of Roman emperors.

Heraldry was a key idiom of Jacobean country house interior decoration,

overleaf *A view towards the oak screen and wainscot panelling of the Marble Hall, a room intended originally for banquets, dances, and masques*

reflecting a family's right to the privileges of inherited rank.[8] At Hatfield the arms of the Cecil family are prominently displayed on the oak screen under the earl's coronet and the family motto: *Sero Sed Serio* (late but in earnest). In 1611 Rowland Buckett was paid for covering the screens with "arms, gilding & personages," including, surprisingly, saints.[9] The oak wainscot panelling is divided into carefully articulated architectural patterns including Doric pilasters, ornamental Flemish strapwork (which was then the height of fashion—often derived from the designs published by Hans Vredeman de Vries), and figurative elements such as the heraldic beasts holding shields.

At the east end of the Marble Hall is the grand staircase, which is a pure piece of Jacobean survival. The open-well staircase was an innovation of this period and provided a considerable opportunity for display and decoration, as can also be seen at Knole in Kent. Here at Hatfield the staircase is crowned with elegantly carved heraldic beasts and putti, with fruits, flowers, and architectural motifs in relief carved by John Bucke. Payments show that the "naked boys and lions holding of instruments and his Lordshyppes arms"[10] were originally part gilded. One of the carved relief panels shows an elegantly dressed gardener at work, thought possibly to be John Tradescant, who travelled to exotic places to collect plants for Cecil's extravagant gardens. The staircase leads to the Great Chamber, known as the King James Drawing Room, which has always been one of the principal rooms of reception.

The room is handsome and large. The centrepiece of the room is undoubtedly the marble chimneypiece carved by Maximilian Colt, over which presides a life-size figure of King James 1 painted to resemble bronze—there can be

The early-seventeenth-century storeyed chimney-pieces in the Long Gallery were painted to resemble stone. The Jacobean plasterwork ceiling was gilded in the nineteenth century.

few more vivid demonstrations of loyalty and devotion to your king. Colt also designed the magnificent tomb to Salisbury in Hatfield Church.

In 1611 the room was described as hung with tapestries showing the story of *Hannibal and Scipio*. The original ceiling was by James Leigh, royal master plasterer, and gilded by Rowland Buckett, with wainscot by Roger Houlton and John Hamond. It has recently been rehung with paintings over tapestry. Now in the Armoury, the domestic organ, delicately painted with flowers and figures by Rowland Buckett, originally stood in this room. The organ's decoration still gives us just a hint of the overall richness of the decorative effect of early-seventeenth-century Hatfield. There are records that Buckett also painted Cecil's bed, chair, and stool with "flowers, birds & personages."11

While furniture, rich tapestry, and other hangings no longer in situ all contributed to the visual vibrancy of the interiors at Hatfield, we can still appreciate the impact of the carved, painted, and inlaid oak wainscot panelling

The King James Drawing Room (the original Great Chamber), over which a life-size bronzed statue of King James I presides. The room has recently been rehung by the present Lord Salisbury, with advice from Alec Cobbe.

that does remain. This is especially noticeable in the immense Long Gallery, a room in late-sixteenth- and early-seventeenth-century country houses set aside for portraits, promenade, and passing the time. In the case of Hatfield the novel contraction of the plan (a U plan rather than the more conventional courtyard plan) made the Long Gallery a circulation space between important apartments. The original plasterwork ceiling (fully gilded only in the nineteenth century) has a cleverly interlaced pattern of decorated ribs that ripple the length of the gallery, while the wainscot panelling by Samuel Jenever has a strongly architectural character with paired Corinthian pilasters at cornice level and inlaid decoration in the main panels framed between Ionic pilasters. The two chimneypieces designed by Jenever are also painted to suggest marble and coloured inlay.

The king's apartment, a suite of rooms culminating originally in an ornate state bed and including "pallet chambers" for servants, lay close to the Great Chamber, while the queen's apartment lay on the corresponding side of the first floor, beside the upper part of Salisbury's breathtaking and extravagant two-storey chapel. For the king's bedchamber an inventory records two sets of bed hangings, one—reserved for the king's use alone—of crimson velvet and white satin embroidered in gold. Robert Cecil's private apartment, including his personal library or "boke chamber" (and a Great Parlour with a fine chimneypiece with his coat of arms), was located on the ground floor below the king's chamber.[12]

Two suites of rooms on the first floor were opened up into large single rooms in the eighteenth and nineteenth centuries, namely those now known

A detail of carved herms in a variegated marble on the impressive chimneypiece by the king's master carver, Flemish-born Maximilian Colt

The Winter Dining Room was created out of two rooms in the nineteenth century. The original Jacobean marble chimneypiece was then moved from another room in the house.

EST·AMOS·PASTOR·HOMINVM

FACTVS

PARCIT·FR VSTRA·JONAS

M·DEVS·

RASCITVR

as the Winter Dining Room (originally probably the suite of rooms for Prince Henry) and the rooms that now form the library (which may have included a state dining room). The Winter Dining Room is now dominated by a vast chimneypiece by Maximilian Colt that was moved here from another room, and the library has a mosaic portrait of Robert Cecil made in Venice in 1608, which previously was sited in the Long Gallery, according to seventeenth-century inventories.[13]

The visual drama of the chapel must have been unexpected even in 1611, with work by all the master craftsmen mentioned above as well as stained-glass artists Louis Dauphin, Martin van Bentheim, and Richard Butler of Southwark. The chapel was mostly redecorated in the early nineteenth century, but the original stained glass, carving, and painted depictions of the apostles survive. Restored after a fire and enriched in the nineteenth century, the chapel is a deeply aesthetic space, in which decoration, gilding, and coloured light all play their roles.[14]

The glory of Hatfield's interior decoration as we see it today, is, of course, not just Jacobean. It owes much to a major campaign of works in the mid-nineteenth century in an antiquarian effort intended to complement and revive the Jacobean character of this great house, and also in the early twenty-first century by the present Marquis of Salisbury. But there can be no doubt that Hatfield is one of the best places to get a sense of the wealth of ambition of the Jacobean court to advance the interests of crown and nation in extravagant building and display, through colour, carving, and light.

The richness of Jacobean Hatfield is reflected in the recent rehang of the picture collection.

2 WILTON HOUSE

The Courtly Caroline Interior

THE HIGH POINT OF INTERIOR DESIGN AND DECORATION IN ENGLAND in the 1630s and '40s must be that associated with Inigo Jones, the first champion of Palladio and the celebrated designer of theatrical masques and court architect. The best surviving example of this period outside a royal palace is found at Wilton House in Wiltshire. The vast south front with the main state rooms was entirely rebuilt in the 1630s for Philip Herbert, the 1st Earl of Montgomery and 4th Earl of Pembroke. He was Lord Chamberlain to Charles I, and his many other offices included Lord Warden of the Stanneries, High Steward of the Duchy of Cornwall, and Vice Admiral of South Wales.[1] Lord

A detail of the carved marble relief over the chimneypiece in the king's bedchamber

37

Pembroke had been a favourite of King Charles's father, James I, with whom he shared a passion for hunting. Inheriting the Wilton estates in 1630, after which his income was calculated to be £30,000 a year, he devoted himself to hunting and the patronage of architecture and painting. According to John Aubrey, he "did not delight in books or poetry; but exceedingly loved painting and building, in which he had singular judgement, and had the best collection of any peer in England, and was a great patron to Sir Anthony Van Dyck."[2]

Inigo Jones was more than instrumental in the 1630s designs. He was by now Surveyor of the King's Works and can be regarded as England's first champion of the Palladian style. In 1612–13 Jones had been on his tour of Italy with the Earl of Arundel, and Arundel had presented Jones with drawings by Palladio and Scammozzi, which became part of his visual armoury. Jones soon established himself as the first champion of the Palladian interpretation of Roman classicism in England, who could draw on his firsthand experience of ancient Roman and sixteenth- and early-seventeenth-century works in Italy. Before working at Wilton, he had nearly completed the Queen's House, Greenwich (1616–35), for Queen Henrietta Maria, and had also designed the magnificent Banqueting House, with its ceiling by Rubens, for Whitehall Palace.

The executant architect at Wilton was a Frenchman, Isaac de Caus, who also designed the formal gardens, with statues and fountains that no longer survive. He had already designed and built the grotto at the Banqueting House in Whitehall under Jones's direction in the mid-1620s. His uncle Salomon had worked for Prince Henry, James I's eldest son, and after 1613 had become

As redesigned by Inigo Jones, the south front of Wilton House, a highly influential classical design in the Palladian spirit. The initial plan was for a range twice the length.

architect to Elector Frederick v of the Palatinate. Jones is known to have annotated designs for the doors and ceilings at Wilton, made by his assistant, John Webb. Aubrey noted in the late seventeenth century that de Caus's work was "not without advice and approbation of Mr Jones."[3]

The ensemble of these great rooms and a state apartment, added to an older house at Wilton, was begun in 1636. They inevitably make a striking contrast to the interiors of Hatfield, completed only twenty years earlier. There, the classical detail was largely decorative in effect, while at Wilton classical detail has been embraced for its proportional values, setting the tone for some of the grandest architectural interiors ever created in England, sourced from the printed treatises of Palladio and the published engravings of French designers, such as Jean Barbet.[4]

According to Aubrey, Charles 1 "did love Wilton above all places: and came thither every sommer." Aubrey also said, "It was he that did put Philip … Earl of Pembroke upon making this magnificent garden and grotto, and to new build that side of the house that fronts the garden, with two stately pavilions at each end all *al Italiano*."[5] It is extraordinary to think that the original plans were yet more ambitious in scale and effect: the south front we see today was only one wing, which would have been repeated on the other side of a central portico (this is known from a drawing by de Caus in the library of Worcester College, Oxford). The scale of this would have been heroic indeed. One wing and the portico were dropped from this plan, with the introduction instead of the stately pavilion end towers, which, it has been suggested, were modelled on the example illustrated in Vincenzo Scammozzi's *Idea dell'Archittetura*

Universale (1615) and were later honoured as a Palladian motif in the eighteenth century.[6]

The surviving interiors of the palatial *piano nobile* of the south front cannot entirely be dated to the project begun in the late 1630s. They belong, to a greater or lesser degree, to a major refurbishment of state rooms after a serious fire of 1647. Although scholars debate what may have survived from the original, there seems no doubt that they were largely redone to the same style. After the fire they seem to have been fully redecorated by the advice of Inigo Jones[11] and, because he was so "very old" by now, they were carried out by his nephew by marriage, Webb, another architect connected to the King's Works.

The six rooms along the south front were intended as a Great Apartment fit for the regular entertainment of the king and queen and the senior members of the court. They form a series of stately rooms of reception that are the architectural and decorative embodiment of the sophisticated, classically inspired world of the Caroline monarchy and aristocracy (as demonstrated in literature and drama). These rooms are marked out by their very proportions as in imitation of Palladio, and the anteroom and vast room originally known as the King's Great Room are in turn known today as the Single Cube Room and the Double Cube Room. Beyond these two spectacular and richly ornamented and gilded rooms lay the suite of the king's bedchamber, with another anteroom, bedchamber, dressing room, and closet.[7]

The original anteroom to the King's Great Room, through which it was approached, is known today as the Single Cube Room. It is some thirty feet high, thirty feet wide, and thirty feet long. The ambition of Pembroke's decoration is seen on glorious early-seventeenth-century coloured arabesque and grotesque work in the twelve-foot cove of the ceiling, painted by Matthew Goodericke. Goodericke also worked in a similar vein on the queen's bedchamber in the Queen's House in Greenwich. The main ceiling painting is

below left A detail of the magnificent ceiling painting in the Single Cube Room by Matthew Goodericke

below right Scenes from Sir Philip Sidney's Arcadia *on the panelling in the Single Cube Room, painted by Emmanuel de Critz*

The Single Cube Room,
with its white painted pine
panelling and elaborate
gilded relief carving
representing drapes, palms,
and swags of fruit

The marble chimneypiece in
the Single Cube Room, based
on an engraving by French
architect Jean Barbet

by Giuseppe Cesari—painted on canvas and acquired in Florence for Lord
Pembroke—and depicts the *Fall of Icarus*. Some have seen it as an allusion to
the fall of Charles I, who had fallen out badly with Pembroke in the 1640s.[8]

Rather unexpected are the twenty-nine scenes from Philip Sidney's *Arcadia*,
painted by Emmanuel de Critz on panels underneath the dado rail. *Arcadia*
was a famous poetical work inspired by the ancient Greek model, with an
idealised account of the life of a shepherd.[9] Sidney was uncle of the 4th Earl,
and his sister was the Countess of Pembroke (indeed, he is said to have written
the poem at Wilton). It was an immensely popular poem, and tradition has it
that Charles I quoted lines from *Arcadia* as he mounted the scaffold.

The overriding character of this room is architectural. Inigo Jones invented
the Palladian interior, for he interpreted the works of Palladio and Vitruvius to
allow for sumptuous interiors and used the drama of Palladio's architectural
repertoire to great effect for interior detail of doorcases and chimneypieces,
articulated within architectural frames with their shaped and open pediments,
all playing their role in articulating the grandeur of the room. The visual centrepiece of the room is the marble chimneypiece inspired by the engravings of
Paris architect Jean Barbet—a favourite source used by Inigo Jones. The walls
are panelled in pine, which was painted white, while the carving and applied
decoration, of crossed palm fronds, faux drapery, and swags of fruit, is gilded
in different shades of gold.

The next room is one with an unparalleled sense of theatre. The Double
Cube Room, sixty feet long, thirty feet wide, and thirty feet high, is simply
huge in scale, twice the length of the Single Cube Room. It is also decorated

overleaf *The Double Cube
Room, originally called "The
King's Great Room," has
white painted panelling with
additional carved and gilded
ornament, and lively trompe
l'oeil ceiling decoration in the
cove by Edward Pearce.*

The main ceiling compartment of the Double Cube Room, painted by Emmanuel de Critz with the legend of Perseus, adding an additional layer of visual fantasy to the room

with a greater degree of richness than the Single Cube, in order to underline its greater status. The architectural quality of the interior decoration is again immediately apparent in the huge doorcases at the eastern end of the room, with its pediments supported by gilded Corinthian pilasters on which recline carved larger-than-life-size figures representing the arts, again fully gilded.

The design of the principal chimneypiece (framed by figures of Bacchus and Ceres) was adapted from exemplars by Barbet, who published his designs for chimneypieces and altarpieces in 1632 and 1641 that had a wide currency throughout Europe—again this underlines the importance of the printed source for English interior decoration. These chimneypieces and doorcases at Wilton were looked to as models by the Palladians of the early eighteenth century.

The principal ceiling painting in this room, by Emmanuel de Critz, Serjeant Painter to Charles I, depicts scenes from the *Legend of Perseus*, the first of the heroes of Greek mythology, who defeated various monsters, including the Medusa, and claimed Andromeda for his wife. The illusionistic presence of a painted dome, part open to the sky in the manner of the Pantheon, adds to the architectural drama of the room. The putti in the coving, depicted as if preparing for a sacrifice or festivity, and the heraldic decoration were painted by Edward Pearce.

John Evelyn mentioned this room in 1654 as "ye dining room in ye modern built part towards the garden richly gilded and painted with story by de Creete."[10] The panelling is adorned with swags of fruit and flowers and classical masks, which echo the garlands depicted in the decoration of the coving. The room is thought to have been somewhat redesigned after the 1647 fire to accommodate a series of Van Dyck portraits of the Herbert family and the royal family, which had previously been hung in Lord Pembroke's London home, Durham House. The room is therefore dominated by the vast group portrait of the Earl of Pembroke and his family, painted by Van Dyck—one of the most glorious group portraits in any English house. It glows with the radiance and colour of their elegant clothing and billowing drapes; the huge scale of the painting makes the figures seem as if they are somehow in the room itself.

It seems strange that the glittering court of King Charles I and his French queen, Henrietta Maria, was utterly overturned by the time the interiors at Wilton were properly finished. Lord Pembroke died in 1649, the same year that his monarch was executed. In fact, he had been dismissed as Lord Chamberlain in 1640, and perhaps surprisingly, having sided with Parliament in the Civil War. This may have been as a result of religious scruple or to preserve his inheritance at Wilton. However, he certainly took a moderate line inclined toward negotiation and distanced himself from the commonwealth government.[11]

Most of the furnishings in the Double Cube Room and the Single Cube Room are early-eighteenth-century pieces designed in Palladian spirit by William Kent for Wanstead and purchased by Catherine Worontzov, Countess of Pembroke, to furnish the state rooms in the 1820s. They still strike an authentically rich note. (The Regency works at Wilton are considered in chapter 11.) What is now known as the Great Ante Room was originally a lobby through which the king's bedchamber was approached. This originally also opened to a staircase, described by Evelyn as "a pair of artificial wynding stairs of stone," which led to the courtyard.[12]

The king's bedchamber comes next, with one of the most delicate of the Barbet-inspired chimneypieces, and the king's dressing room, now known as the Corner Room, with another of the elegant marble chimneypieces. Like a private withdrawing room to the state suite, the Corner Room was always filled with the choicest pictures, and Inigo Jones referred to it as the "cabinet" for this reason. It still contains some of the finest smaller paintings in the collection. The last and smallest of the state rooms, the intimate king's closet, served as the king's inner retreat and was linked to a private back staircase for access by trusted servants. These rooms were redecorated by Andien de Clermont in the 1730s with delightful ceilings. Other private drawing rooms that date back to the seventeenth century include the Hunting Room, with panels depicting hunting scenes painted in the 1650s by Edward Pierce.

The Double Cube Room was described by John Cornforth in *English Country Houses: Caroline* as "without question the noblest room of the period"[13] and is certainly one of the most impressive and stately rooms in any English country house. A room designed for the reception of the monarch, it has been used in its time as dining room, drawing room, and ballroom, and has, along with the whole house, been carefully redecorated and the furnishings newly presented by the current Earl and Countess of Pembroke.[14]

The carved and gilded overmantel in the king's bedchamber. H stands for Herbert, P for Pembroke, and M for Montgomery.

3 BOUGHTON HOUSE

The Taste for France

IN THE LATE SEVENTEENTH CENTURY THE EXTRAORDINARY RICHNESS and drama of the French court at Versailles inevitably inspired imitation all around Europe—and Protestant England was not immune. No country house owner was more likely to imitate this style than Ralph Montagu (created 1st Earl of Montagu in 1689 and 1st Duke in 1705, here referred to as the 1st Duke).[1] This was first because of his exceptional cultivation and interest in the fine and decorative arts, and second for the more practical reason that he had served as an ambassador to the court of Louis XIV in the 1660s and '70s. The young Montagu was deeply impressed by the sheer glamour and *gloire* of

A detail of boullework on the long case clock of the 1690s in the state withdrawing room at Boughton House

51

The arcade of the new range designed and built from 1683 onwards for Ralph Montagu, 1st Duke of Montagu, who had served as ambassador to the court of Louis XIV

Versailles and was determined to bring something of that back to the English court as a matter of patriotic duty. As Boyer wrote in 1713, it was from visits to Versailles and St. Cloud "that his Grace formed his Ideas in his own Mind, of both Buildings and Gardening."[2] The 1st Duke brought contemporary French style to bear not only on Montagu House, his London palace, but also at Boughton House, his Northamptonshire country seat, from 1684—the furnishing was intended for the reception of William III as well as ambassadors from the French court. Montagu's influence grew through his role, from 1671, as Master of the Great Wardrobe, responsible for decorating and furnishing royal palaces. He also acquired the Mortlake tapestry workshop from Lord Brouncker in 1674, where he probably intended to commission copies of the Gobelins tapestries in England for the benefit of court taste in England.

However, by the 1680s the 1st Duke was out of favour as an opponent of the accession of the Catholic James II and lost his post at court. He spent the years 1682–85 in France before returning from exile to retirement "in the enjoyment of a Fine family and flowing Fortune, and this time he spent in Building two very magnificent Structures for his own Residence."[3] He regained the Great Wardrobe position when William III and Mary II came to power in 1689. Thus we can see that the lustre of French glamour in decoration superseded problematic Catholic associations, as can also be seen when William III commissioned Talman to design a French-inspired Trianon at Hampton Court, despite being a sworn enemy of Louis XIV.

Montagu House, the 1st Duke's town house, was the envy of London. In the 1670s, he had employed Verrio, the Italian painter, to paint its ceilings with

Boughton House, seen from the west (only the north range was completed for the 1st Duke of Montagu)

mythological subjects, which are thought to have initiated the fashion for such decoration in late-seventeenth-century England. In the 1680s he employed two French painters, La Fosse and Rousseau, to produce new ceilings after a fire there. John Evelyn wrote of Montagu House that for painting and furniture "there was nothing more glorious in England."[4] The architect of Montagu House is not known, although in *Vitruvius Britannicus* Colen Campbell attributes the design to a Mr. Pouget, whereas more recently scholars, such as Gervase Jackson-Stops, have suggested the hand of Daniel Marot "the spider at the centre of this web of Huguenot activity,"[5] which included the cabinetmaker Gole, Marot's brother-in-law. Whoever was his chief architect, there can be no doubt that the 1st Duke gathered into his service many of the leading craftsmen, often French Huguenots, who could help him realise his ambitions. This included painters such as Chéron, who had trained under Charles Le Brun at the French Academy, and carvers and gilders such as the Pelletiers. The ceilings painted by Cheron are his largest surviving recorded commission.

At Boughton, the 1st Duke extended his existing house to the north, providing a magnificent suite of new state apartments on the first floor, with two pavilions containing suites (of which he completed only one). He also transformed the Great Hall, giving it a huge coved and painted ceiling, decorated by Chéron. The first-floor state rooms are approached by a magnificent stone staircase with a wrought-iron balustrade.[6]

The decoration of the staircase hall is realised in paint. In the lower part of the staircase hall, the walls are painted to suggest rustication, which is a French technique, while the first-floor level is painted in trompe l'oeil with niches for

sculpture and reliefs based on engravings from the frieze of the Dacian captives on the Arch of Constantine in Rome. The single figure within a niche is the allegorical figure *Abundance*. The cornice combines three-dimensional and painted details.

The ceiling by Chéron depicts *The Banquet of the Gods at the Marriage of Peleus and Thetis*. This is the first scene in the story of the Judgement of Paris, with the god Mercury being despatched to find a mortal judge to decide which of the three goddesses is most beautiful. In the 1680s Chéron was considered as important a painter as Verrio and Laguerre, and deserves greater recognition. His ceilings at Boughton are all painted with mythological scenes drawn from Ovid's *Metamorphoses*, probably chosen by the 1st Duke himself and painted in a manner suggestive of Chéron's time studying in Italy. The coves, usually painted in trompe l'oeil architecture showing stone balustrades, create an enticing layer of fantasy architecture through which the god-filled skies can be glimpsed full of colour and activity, with subjects that might well have suggested specific political allusions at the time.

The ceiling of the first state room depicts *Venus Interceding for Aeneas*, which shows the goddess asking Jupiter for Aeneas's safe passage to Italy so he could found the Roman empire. The ceiling of the room now known as the second state room illustrates *The Fall of Pyrenes*, another tale from Ovid about a tyrant filled with pride who eventually falls to Earth; this has been taken to be a reference to the fall of James II.[7] For all his love of French splendour, the 1st Duke was an ardent Protestant and vigorously opposed the accession of a Roman Catholic monarch.

A gilded candle stand in the first state room

Other ceilings of course are more straightforward: the ceiling of the state bedchamber shows Venus and Mars caught in Vulcan's net, a suitably amorous subject for a bedroom, however grand. It symbolises the crowning power of Cupid's love. The bed on which they lie is held up by putti, and Chéron has created an eye-catching contrast in Venus's pale flesh against Vulcan's ruddiness.

Painted decoration aside, nowhere in England is it possible to encounter so much late-seventeenth-century furniture and textiles surviving in their original context as at Boughton. The state rooms or Great Apartment were almost complete in October 1695, when visited by William III. From the top of the staircase you can look through to an enfilade of the king's dining room, withdrawing room, state bedchamber, and cabinet. The enfilade was designed as a processional route, and the richness and quality of the furnishings and hangings increase the further the visitor passes along.[8]

The windows along the enfilade are all on the north side, and Versailles parquet flooring is laid throughout—an early example, in England, of this technique in a country house. The rooms are panelled with moulded frames creating compartments: on the proportional model of a column, the main panel being the column element, the dado being the plinth, and the frieze, the cornice. The "drab green" paint colour in the first state room seems to be one of the few genuine survivals of a Baroque colour scheme. The subsequent rooms were hung with tapestries. Each room has a bolection-moulded chimneypiece of different coloured marbles. An inventory of 1697 shows that the state rooms were mostly hung with tapestries illustrating the Acts of the Apostles, woven at the Mortlake workshops. Boughton has two sets of these tapestries, woven in the 1630s and 1670s, both based on the Raphael cartoon of the same subject that had been acquired by King Charles I.

The first state room served as the king's dining room. In the late seventeenth century, dining was still very much a moveable feast: chairs would have been moved around as needed and ranged against the walls when not

The enfilade through the main state apartment on the piano nobile, *with the original parquet floor in imitation of that in Versailles and the original late-seventeenth-century paint colour*

A detail of one of the Acts of the Apostles *tapestries woven in Mortlake, after the cartoons by Raphael. This one hangs in the High Pavilion Bedroom and depicts Elymas struck by blindness.*

needed. After the service of meals, tea might be taken. The dark japanned chairs are thought to be those originally supplied for the room.[9] In the second state room (the withdrawing room) are two tapestries, one showing *The Death of Ananias*, and the other *The Sacrifice at Lystra*. The late-seventeenth-century walnut chairs are upholstered in crimson velvet and, when lined against the wall, show how the moveable furniture played its part in the interior styling of rooms. It meant that whole screens of colour and texture could be manipulated throughout the suite of rooms. The tripartite sets of matching marquetry table, mirrors, and candle stands on the north wall are another characteristic example of the treatment of groups of furnishings in the seventeenth-century aristocratic interior.

The visual climax of a Great Apartment was always the state bed; the one at Boughton has recently been loaned back from the Victoria and Albert Museum after a long and complex programme of restoration. The bed, hung with rich crimson damask, gold brocading, and ostrich feathers, stands back from the enfilade and can only be seen by those given permission to enter the bedchamber itself—of privileged access only. It was described in the 1697 inventory as "A Crimson gold flowered damask bed" accompanied by "6 Earme Chayers japand black covered with ye seame damask."[10]

The room beyond is the cabinet room, a yet more private retreat. Early inventories suggest that the room was originally hung in a blue and silver damask (it is described as "the Blew damask drawing room" in 1697), which

right The state bed at Boughton, recently returned to the house from the Victoria and Albert Museum. Its original damask and gold brocade has been conserved to recapture the original richness of effect.

below left Late-seventeenth-century walnut chairs upholstered in their original crimson velvet

below right A detail of the ceiling painting in the state bedchamber by Louis Cheron shows Venus and Mars, with Venus painted in such a way that she seems to stand up as the viewer passes through the room

overleaf left A table arranged for the service of tea with original ladderback chairs

overleaf right Four upholstered chairs with original late-seventeenth-century upholstery. It is thought that the formal state withdrawing room was once hung in blue damask similar to the chair at top right.

is thought to be that found on an upholstered stool and armchair in the next room. The ceiling shows *Jupiter Restraining Arcas from Shooting at the Bear Callisto*.

An unexpected contrast is found in the library, which has a more anti-quarian character, panelled in the 1620s. The 1st Duke's family tree is carved over the chimneypiece tracing the family's descent from William I to the 2nd Duke's marriage to Mary Churchill. A similar heraldic display is found in the Little Hall, which was formed to create a lobby between the remodelled Great Hall and the garden and staircase hall. The ceiling of the Little Hall was painted by Chéron to show *The Return of Proserpine*.

The 1st Duke re-created the Great Hall of the former hunting lodge into a banqueting hall in the "antique" manner. He added Ionic pilasters to sup-port the vaulted ceiling concealing the original hammer-beam roof above it. The ceiling painting depicts *The Banquet of the Gods and the Marriage of Hercules*, the heroic mortal whose virtue allowed him into communion with the gods (the ceiling includes his marriage to the goddess Hebe). This was commissioned in 1705. Here Chéron used Charles Le Brun's ceiling of the *Gallerie d'Apollon* in the Louvre as his model, especially for the dramatic revelation of the light of day, as Apollo brings daylight in his chariot. The ceiling of the adjoining eating room has *The Triumph of Bacchus and Ariadne*.

The 1st Duke was a noted host, witty and genial. The French philosopher St. Evremond wrote that his greatest pleasure was to visit Boughton and to be "with my Lord Montagu, to enjoy his conversation twice a day, before and after the best cheer in the world."[11] William Congreve dedicated *The Way of the World* to him in 1699: "If I am not mistaken, poetry is almost the only art which has not yet laid claim to your Lordship's patronage. Architecture and painting, to the great honour of our country, have flourished under your influence and patronage."[12] We must imagine a man interested in every detail.

Yet more poignant perhaps today is the remarkable survival here at Boughton of late-seventeenth-century furniture, of leading French and English manufacture, that was supplied for this house and for the 1st Duke's other houses, by André Boulle, Pierre Gole, and Gerrit Jensen, among others. The ornate gilt furniture and rich upholstery, combined with the energetic activity of gods on every ceiling of significance, is suggestive of the classical poetic tradition of the communion between gods and heroic mortals to which the 1st Duke and his cultivated guests would have been sensitive. The rooms at Boughton are the symbolic meeting place.

Beautifully preserved through the twentieth century by the present Duke and his parents and grandparents, the interiors of Boughton have long been admired as one of England's sleeping beauties. A visit here is, as eminent furniture historian John Hardy has observed, "primarily a journey through a seventeenth-century re-creation of the classical world,"[13] which evokes the direct influence of Versailles on English interior decoration.

A very rare 1690s glass single candlearm of great simplicity

4 CHATSWORTH

The English Baroque Interior

CHATSWORTH IN DERBYSHIRE IS AMONG THE MOST FAMOUS OF
country houses and one of the most important Baroque houses in England.
The original house built by Bess of Hardwick was a substantial Elizabethan
hunting lodge, constructed around a courtyard that was transformed, with
interiors of Baroque theatricality, in stages over some twenty years by William
Cavendish, the 4th Earl of Devonshire (who in 1694 was created 1st Duke).[1]

The 1st Duke's work on the house began in 1687 with Rome-trained William
Talman, one of the leading architects of the day and the Comptroller of the
King's Works who had worked with Sir Christopher Wren on Hampton

*A bronze and marble bust
of Louis XIV in Chatsworth's
state music room*

67

Court. A Whig in politics and a champion of the Protestant succession, the 1st Duke was one of the seven noblemen who invited William and Mary to the throne. He was immediately appointed Lord Steward and was at first an influential figure of William and Mary's government.

In effect, the 1st Duke rebuilt his Derbyshire seat to be a suitable place to entertain his monarchs, who were themselves notable patrons of architecture (although it seems that they never actually came to Chatsworth). The 1st Duke nevertheless employed many of the craftsmen associated with William and Mary's work at Hampton Court to create some of the most lavish interiors in England, reflecting ducal magnificence from the start.[2]

Like the Duke of Montagu at Boughton, the 1st Duke was also influenced by the court of the Catholic monarch Louis XIV and had been to Versailles on embassy in 1669. He not only employed artists and craftsmen who had worked there, but also possibly modelled the west front of Chatsworth on the example of Louis's chateau at Marly, designed by Mansart and Charles Le Brun. William III had an engraving of this chateau hanging in his cabinet at Hampton Court.

The core of the theatrical splendour of Chatsworth is found, unusually, three storeys up, where Talman designed a state apartment on the south front that replaced the old Long Gallery of the courtly Elizabethan house, meaning that the *piano nobile* was above the family apartments. A state apartment would more usually be found on the first storey. The state apartment at Chatsworth was designed to have a sequence of magnificent rooms of reception, in which, as at Boughton, painted ceilings of carefully chosen mythological subjects,

Chatsworth, viewed from across the park, as rebuilt for the 1st Duke from the 1680s. To the left are additions for the 6th Duke.

tapestries, rich textiles, and upholstered furniture played a critical role in creating visual sensation. Such rooms are interior design at its most deliberate and seductive. The expenditure could be colossal.

A recent restoration program (of 2005–07, initiated by the 12th Duke) has refocussed the display of these rooms on the furnishing of the 1st Duke's time, re-creating arrangements of furniture and tapestries to help recapture the essential Baroque flavour of the house.[3] However, a precise re-creation was not possible, as many of the original furnishings had been removed to different rooms, particularly in the nineteenth century, when much of the Baroque furniture was moved to Hardwick Hall.

The 1st Duke's architect, Talman, built up the visual effect in preparation for the state apartment from the courtyard, from which the house was entered in the late seventeenth century. From this first moment the richness and extravagance of detail was uppermost, as can be seen in the classical trophies

of arms, carved by Samuel Watson, signifying peace following armed conflict. Watson was the principal carver at Chatsworth who worked here for more than twenty years. These trophies were immediately echoed in the elegant painted decoration.[4] The visitor would then pass first into the double-height Painted Hall, formerly the Great Hall of the Elizabethan house, which would still have been seen as a great banqueting hall in the 1680s and '90s. Inside the Painted Hall, the painted decoration covers both walls and ceiling of intentional magnificence. Louis Laguerre, a French decorative artist who had worked at Versailles, was commissioned to paint *The Life of Julius Caesar*. This included the assassination of Caesar led by Brutus, which is now thought to be a direct allusion to the bringing down of the autocratic leader, thus celebrating William's role in ousting his own father-in-law, James II. Brutus was a hero to the Whigs for his role in protecting the constitution of Rome against the overweening pride of Ceasar, declaring himself in effect king. The 1st Duke's own monument in Derby refers to his personal role as "an enemy to tyrants."[5]

The first staircase here originally was in a doubled, curved form. The present staircase, which today somewhat dominates the room, dates to 1912. The ironwork balustrades carefully match those of the original Baroque work.

A detail of the carving by Samuel Watson, full of life and delicacy

This staircase leads through a triumphal arch to a first floor, from which level the Great Staircase rises. Behind the hall staircase is an elegant grotto, with a fine marble relief of the Roman goddess Diana bathing. The Great Staircase, which leads to the state apartment, is approached through the triumphal arch motif. It was something of an engineering triumph for the time, as the steps were cantilevered "so artfully contriv'd that they seem to hang in the air."[6] The stairs, with a balustrade by John Gardom, also have fine gilded wrought-iron panels made by Jean Tijou, a Huguenot master blacksmith who is thought to have trained at Versailles and came to England to work for William and Mary at Hampton Court. The 1st Duke appears to have begun with the intention of having the walls fully painted. Then he resolved to have sculpture by Cibber displayed in niches, with carved swags and garlands of flowers and fruit that match elements of Verrio's dramatic ceiling, showing *The Fall of Phaeton*.

At the top of the staircase is first the Great Chamber, another room of assembly and display where members of the household and other visitors would have gathered to attend on the visiting monarchs. This was probably also used as a dining room, and in the 2005–07 redisplay, an elegant buffet display of food, flowers, Oriental porcelain, and silver gilt was created to capture the richness of the original Baroque luxury. Again, we meet here the theme of heroic and virtuous mortals dining in the presence of the gods. The painted ceiling is a vigorous display of movement of gods within a sky, painted by Verrio in 1691–92, representing the story of *The Return to the Golden Age*, with Vices destroyed by Virtues. This is thought to be a direct celebration of the Glorious Revolution and the achievement of William III and Mary II.[7]

The walls are panelled in oak, on which there was also additional decoration in delicate lime-wood carvings by Samuel Watson, of swags of fish, game, and flowers—clearly the equal to that of the better-known Grinling Gibbons. These carvings would originally have been much paler in contrast with the oak, almost silvery in colour, a contrast that was picked up in the colours of

The newly installed buffet display in the Great Chamber, presented in the late-seventeenth-century manner with fruit, flowers, Oriental porcelain, and silver gilt plate to suggest the 1st Duke's wealth and good taste

overleaf *The state drawing room, with an ornately carved overmantel frame and a cabinet on legs made for the 1st Duke from Coromandel lacquer. Porcelain has been arranged in the late-seventeenth-century manner.*

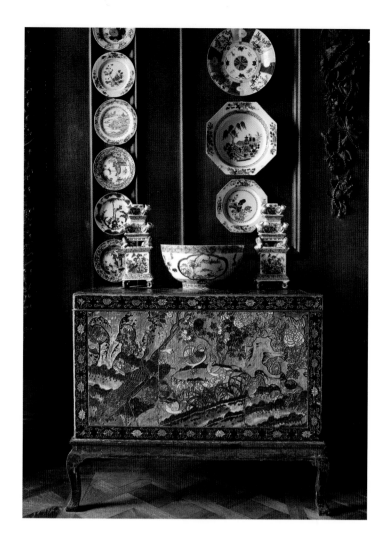

the painted frieze. As at Boughton, the floors are in parquet on the model of Versailles. To add to the visual effect of the interiors, the doors to the state apartment line up in sequence along the enfilade, a typical Baroque motif that was dominant in French architecture and much imitated in England (and artfully extended by a large mirror at one end). As at Boughton, through the evidence of surviving decoration and inventory, we can see how the rooms of the state apartment become more sumptuous. Each room was accessible only by an increasingly select few, as they approached the more private rooms occupied by the monarchs (although they were more public than our modern concept of privacy would allow).[8]

Next comes the state withdrawing room, where the first rank of privileged courtiers and visitors would be allowed access. In this room hang the Mortlake tapestries of the *Life of the Apostles*, based on the cartoons by Raphael, which we also encountered at Boughton, and which are thought to have hung in this room since the eighteenth century. In 2005–07 cabinets on stands and treasured porcelain vases were positioned in the spirit of Baroque interior decoration, modelled on paintings of the time and inventory evidence, using furniture from the collection. Porcelain and pottery with their never-fading flowers had an important role in the Baroque interior. The hearth when not in use would have its slab decked with vases and tubs for orange trees and roses.

After that comes the anteroom to the state bedchamber (known since the early nineteenth century as the state music room, when it was hung in stamped leather by the 6th Duke, whose considerable contribution to other rooms at Chatsworth will be discussed in chapter 10). In both rooms we find the typical

Baroque layered richness, including panelling with inlaid and carved decoration, different coloured bolection-moulded marble chimneypieces, carved wooden cornices, and painted trompe l'oeil architecture by Laguerre above, the detail in the frieze in particular painted in a heightened relief with vivid shadow and almost mobile figures.

The state bedchamber was the visual climax of the state rooms, with the richest concentration of textures in materials such as silk damask, gilding, and upholstered furniture, as well as costly mirror glass. An early inventory listed "one fine Lookg Glass betwixt ye Windows, a marble slab on an iron frame … the Hang of this Room is Tapestry." The looking glass in the state bedchamber was made in 1703 by John Gumley with blue glass and the 1st Duke's insignia of the Garter.[9] The diarist Celia Fiennes visited Chatsworth in 1697 and described the state apartment as it was then newly completed: "all painted very finely on the top … there was sweete tapestry hangings with small figures and very much silke, they look'd as fresh as if new, tho' bought severall years [ago], there were no beds up."[10] This shows a contemporary's reaction to the original presentation of the rooms and the expectation that the state bed would usually be the most magnificent element. These rooms seemed tired and gloomy a few decades later, when Horace Walpole wrote that every room seemed "sombre,"[11] and by the early nineteenth century the 6th Duke called it a "museum of old furniture, and a walk in bad weather."[12] But these comments reflect changes in taste and attitude as much as anything else.

The state bed shown here is not the original bed supplied for the room, but is one of appropriate date. The state bed was conserved in 2005–07, heightened

The magnificent state bed, recently conserved. This was not the original bed for this room, but one of a similar date. Recent conservation included returning the tester to its original height.

The fireplaces are filled with Delft earthenware vases and flowers in the manner that can be observed in late-seventeenth-century paintings

overleaf *The extraordinary range of decorative effect at Chatsworth is shown in painting, sculpture, and wood carving, bringing colour and theatre to these ducal interiors*

and the original hangings carefully preserved. Silk damask was rewoven on the advice of Annabel Westman to be used for the curtains. Tapestries were rehung here, and a collection of old master paintings concentrated in this room helped to revive the sense of elite magnificence aimed at by Talman and the 1st Duke in the late seventeenth century. The next room is a small, private closet, the final withdrawing room of the monarch, often hung as we have seen with the finest small pictures or other treasures. This was originally panelled in rare and expensive imported lacquer, known as Coromandel, later removed by the 1st Duke and used to create coffers, one of which can be seen in the room today, and two others in the state drawing room. It was a room of the moment, as Oriental style was increasingly popular as a result of the activities of the East India Company, hence also the presence of so much exceptional porcelain in these rooms. The 1st Duke also had a grand receiving room west of the state apartment painted by Sir James Thornhill showing *The Rape of the Sabines*, which refers to the Duke's role in the creation of the United Kingdom. This served, in effect, as another anteroom to suites of other guests' apartments on this floor.

On the ground floor, the double-height chapel is one of the best preserved of the late-seventeenth-century spaces at Chatsworth. Completed in 1693, it is at first glance so richly Baroque in character that it seems an unlikely chapel for the house of the leading champion of the Protestant cause.[13] But on closer inspection, the chapel's iconography is self-consciously Protestant, with the alabaster figures of Faith and Justice, sculpted by Cibber, instead of saints, and the arrangement of the altar with a reading table and no cross. The swags and putti on the wainscot panelling were carved in fragrant cedar by Samuel Watson. The ceiling is painted with *The Resurrected Christ in All His Glory* by Laguerre, and scenes from *The Life of Christ* on the walls. A painting of *Doubting Thomas* by Verrio is framed in the alabaster reredos.

Chatsworth preserves interiors of staggering richness of detail, and despite the alterations and additions of centuries, this remains one of the places in England where one can observe the flavour of the English version of the Baroque. Defoe called it "a Palace for a Prince, a most magnificent beauty."[14] The recent restoration programme for the 12th Duke and the Chatsworth House Trust, advised by their own curatorial team, and also by Peter Inskip, Jonathan Bourne, and David Mlinaric, has allowed the late-seventeenth-century interiors to be appreciated in their period character.[15]

A detail of the cedarwood carving in the chapel

5 CASTLE HOWARD

The Imagination of Vanbrugh

CASTLE HOWARD IN YORKSHIRE IS AMONG THE GREAT HOUSES OF THE
English Baroque, the first work of Sir John Vanbrugh, one of the most ingenious architects of the early eighteenth century. It was begun in 1699 for
Charles Howard, the 3rd Earl of Carlisle, who was in 1701–02 the First Lord
of the Treasury to William III. He was effectively leader of the government, a
position he enjoyed again in 1715 for George I, after which he was succeeded by
Sir Robert Walpole. An enormously ambitious house in spirit, Castle Howard
was, as with Boughton and Chatsworth, influenced by French country house
planning and, more important, by an idealised vision of ancient Rome and
ancient Roman mythology.[1]

*A detail of the gilded ironwork
of the gallery overlooking the
Great Hall*

Castle Howard was the first English country house to be built with a dome, which not only dominates the skyline of both north and south elevations but creates a most exciting and theatrical interior space: the Great Hall. Vanbrugh, a soldier and playwright with no known background in architecture, wisely employed the highly experienced Nicholas Hawksmoor as his assistant (as he also would at Blenheim). Hawksmoor, who had been Sir Christopher Wren's principal assistant for many years, must have helped Vanbrugh in most aspects of the design.[2]

Hawksmoor certainly defended the choice to have a Doric order to the north (on the model, he said, of Inigo Jones's and John Webb's work at Greenwich Palace) and the more palatial Corinthian order to the expansive south front. The 3rd Earl also developed with these two men a highly sophisticated park landscape with a series of temples, lead sculptures by Andries Carpentière and John van Nost, and castellated enclosures, which all underline the evocation of the Arcadian classical world encountered throughout the house.

The north entrance front of the house with its *corps de logis*—wings connected to a central range by curved arcades—has paired Doric pilasters, banded rustication, and numerous classical figures of the muses. The whole makes what Vanbrugh was to praise elsewhere as "a very Noble and masculine Shew."[3] The east wing (described in 1725 as "the useful part where the family live") was completed in 1705, followed by the main range, while the west wing was planned in detail but never in fact executed to Vanbrugh's plan.[4] A west wing was built but to a new plan by Palladian architect Sir Thomas Robinson, who also planned to recase the whole in more sober Palladian style.

A view into the dome over the Great Hall, as restored after a fire in 1940, showing The Fall of Phaeton

The interiors of Vanbrugh's building combine theatrical magnificence with a surprising degree of intimacy. The extraordinary Great Hall, thirty-five feet square, rises seventy feet through two storeys to a dome supported by a lantern through which light floods down. The staircases on either side are open to the hall, creating further angles and shadows to this remarkable space. In this room, painted decoration was used to maximum possible effect.

The 3rd Earl was a significant patron of two of the most important Italian decorative painters at work in England: Gianantonio Pellegrini and Marco Ricci, both from Venice. Pellegrini painted the staircase walls as well as the pendentives and dome of the Great Hall, while Marco Ricci painted a series of genre scenes for the overdoors. Vanbrugh must have recommended the two painters, for he had employed them for scene painting for opera in London, as he tried in these years to introduce Italian opera to an English audience. (Other paintings by Ricci have been hung in the Castle Howard bedroom since 1993). Ricci was paid £100 for his work there in 1709–10[5]; the 3rd Earl probably also acquired flower paintings by Monnoyer.

The interior of the dome of the Great Hall was painted with *The Fall of Phaeton*. A surprisingly popular subject in country house ceiling decoration (as for instance at Chatsworth), the iconographic interpretation is open to debate, as Phaeton's downfall is often seen as the result of vanity—the downfall of pride. However, Charles Saumarez-Smith in *The Building of Castle Howard* (1990) has suggested that it was intended rather to bring to mind Ovid's vivid and imaginative description of Phaeton's visit to Apollo, his reputed father, in the Palace of the Sun.

The top-lit Great Hall is a very dramatic interior, with a deliberately theatrical architectural framework

It is a dazzling description: "Sol's loftie Palace on high Pillars rais'd, / Shone all with gold, and stones that flamelike blaz'd. / The roofe of Ivory, divinely deckt: / The two-leav'd silver doores bright raise project / The workmanship more admiration crav'd: / For curious Mulciber has there ingrav'd / The Land-imbracing Sea, the orbed Ground, / The arched Heavens, Blew Gods the billowes crown'd."[6] This is probably one of the most suggestive descriptions of a palace in classical literature. Lord Carlisle owned more editions and translations of Ovid's *Metamorphoses* than of any other book in his library.

Apollo, the god of the sun, was the source of life and light as well as the god of arts, poetry, and music, and thus leader of the muses (and associated with festivities too). Depicted as an idealised beautiful youth, athletic and beardless, Apollo is one of the gods (originally Greek, adopted by the Roman world) most widely represented in late-seventeenth- and early-eighteenth-century interior iconography.

Most important, Apollo was the favoured device of Louis XIV, and every room at Versailles, the most admired palace of the time, was touched with his image. As a contemporary guidebook for Versailles put it: "there is nothing in this amazing house which is not associated with that divinity; every single figure and every ornament that you see there is not placed by accident."[7] The latter remark could also be said of Castle Howard, although this was no intentional homage to Louis, as the 3rd Earl was one of the leading Whigs of the day.

The whole universe is alluded to in the iconography of the painted decoration: day and light in the Great Hall; Air, Fire, Earth, and Water on the pendentives below the dome; and Apollo and the Muses, Apollo and Midas,

and depictions of the continents on the staircase walls. The paintings present within the architectural space a cosmology of continents, elements, music, and the firmament.

Night and Sleep were also depicted by Pellegrini in the Grand Cabinet at the west end of the south front. The story of *Endymion and Diana* was depicted by Pellegrini: Endymion was a mortal shepherd asleep on Mount Latmos, with whom Diana fell in love, and in revenge for their association for just one night, Jupiter condemned him to perpetual sleep. (This room was demolished in the 1720s when the west wing was being built to designs by Sir Thomas Robinson.) This is another story of mortals brought close to communion with the gods (if only briefly), which is characteristic of the decorative painting of the interiors of the late seventeenth and early eighteenth centuries in particular.[8]

It is interesting to see how the Great Hall sets the theatrical tone for the house, while the rooms on the south front—though arranged on impressive enfilades that originally reached to either end of the whole front, on two storeys—were relatively intimate spaces. The hall is a truly multilayered interior, of a type unparalleled in English domestic architecture, and it is often compared to the crossing of a great church in Paris or Rome. The space brings together an entrance hall with two grand Baroque staircase apartments that are partly open to the central, full-height space under the dome, thus merging for the visitor all the rich and thrilling decoration into a spectacular unity.

Two long corridors on the north and south sides of the house intersect with the hall. The vaulted corridors furnished natural sculpture galleries for the collections, mostly made by Carlisle's son and heir, the 4th Earl, while he

left A detail of one of the richly carved Corinthian capitals in the Great Hall

right Details of the stuccowork overmantel frame and the painted musical trophy

was on his Grand Tour. The 4th Earl also collected paintings by Canaletto, Pannini, and Zucarelli.

The staircases and galleries that cross the hall offer the visitor an up-close demonstration of classical detail and mythological exposition. It almost resembles a stage set of a palace, in which meals might be taken and music performed; as Geoffrey Beard observes in *The Work of John Vanbrugh*: "the giant orders of the piers and the painted dome were in one splendid gesture—worthy to be a stage set by Ferdinando Bibiena for the Hapsburgs in Vienna."[9] Although there is no documentary evidence, the presence of the musical trophies in the decoration seems to indicate that the room might have been used for musical performances, at least in the mind of Vanbrugh.

The painting inside the dome itself is a modern re-creation after a major fire in 1940 destroyed the dome and most of the main first-floor rooms. The lost rooms included the High Saloon, which had a ceiling by Pellegrini depicting Minerva and Venus, and the walls around the room showed events from the story of the Trojan War.

One of the innovations at Castle Howard can be found in the very fine plasterwork by the Italian stuccadore Giovanni Bagutti and his assistant Giuseppe Plura, who created the extraordinary overmantel frame in the Great Hall, surrounding a depiction of Vulcan. The elegant stuccowork includes two winged herms supporting baskets of flowers, with tails terminating in scrolled conches and cascades of flowers—one of the finest pieces of plasterwork in any English house at this date. The bolection-moulded chimneypiece in the hall was in a coloured scagliola, as was the 1711–12 niche for classical sculpture

The original enfilade, as
seen from the Crimson Dining
Room looking towards the
Garden Hall

(now framing a figure of Bacchus) that faces it—these are early examples of
the use of scagliola in England. Other exuberant overdoors are only recorded
in photographs.

Stone carving and woodcarving also played important roles in the interiors
of Castle Howard, following the richness of carving of the entrance front.
This was carried out by Samuel Carpenter of York, and the Huguenot refugee
Nadauld, who also worked at Chatsworth. Their work includes the handsome
layered cornices with paired scrolled brackets in the music room and the
Crimson Dining Room. Delicate and highly decorative, they were intended
to frame tapestries and damask hangings. Grinling Gibbons was also paid for
work here in 1705–06, and an overdoor in the Crimson Dining Room is attrib-
uted to him still.

Textiles were key, and although few of the original hangings survive at
Castle Howard, there is telling evidence in inventories. As early as May 1706
John Vanderbank was paid for tapestries for "the App[artment] of State,"
which probably referred to the 3rd Earl's bedchamber in the east wing. In a
later inventory the bed was described as hung with "Crimson Flowers & silver
Tissue Ground" and the tapestry described as having "Tartary & Chinese
Figures."[10] In 1732 John Tracy Atkyns described the tapestries as having
a "very beautiful mixture of colours, Chinese men & women in variety of
postures all sorts of birds, beasts & fish." Vanderbank also supplied tapestries
for other rooms.

The drawing room in the southeast wing was originally hung in blue caffoy;
the bedchamber curtains in crimson silk damask; the dressing rooms with
lustring, a shiny, crisp, specially treated silk; and "My Lord Grand's Cabinet"
with green mohair. The state drawing room at the west end was hung with blue
velvet, with "14 very large silver sconces," while the state bed was hung with
"Gold laced" crimson velvet and more tapestries by Vanderbank of *The Seasons*.
The contrasts in colours and richness have been reproduced in spirit in late-
twentieth-century redecorations.

Despite the obvious ostentation of the hall and the grandeur of the enfilade
of the state rooms on the south front, it is clear that Vanbrugh cared about
the comfort of the houses he built. He wrote about Castle Howard to another
client: "For, tho' we have now as bitter storms as rain and wind can well
compose, every room in the house is like an oven, and in corridors of 200 ft.
long there is not air in motion to stir the flame of a candle."[11]

The 1940 fire devastated the interiors of a large portion of the south front
on the ground and first floors, but enough survives on the western end to
show the carved doorcases and chimneypieces of Vanbrugh's era, and to show
the surprising intimacy of the state apartments as conceived by Vanbrugh
and Carlisle—and executed by English, French, and Italian craftsmen.
Inventories show that there were numerous marble-topped tables (the marble
from Derbyshire and Italy), walnut furniture, gilded pier glasses, and upholstered chairs.[12] While these rooms are filled with late-eighteenth- and early-
ninteenth century furniture today, they still suggest the same degree of almost
intoxicating richness, due to programmes of redecoration and restoration by
the late Lord Howard and his son, the Hon. Simon Howard.

6 HOUGHTON HALL

The Palladian Interior I

BY THE EARLY 1720S THE WORLD OF ENGLISH INTERIOR DESIGN HAD shifted a key, as the enjoyable richness and vibrancy of the Baroque was subjected to the new aesthetic demands of the Palladian movement. As noted in chapter 2, the Palladian style had first been introduced to England by Inigo Jones one hundred years before but received a new impetus in the 1720s, as Lord Burlington and others championed the works of Palladio as the touchstone of taste.[1]

Houghton Hall in Norfolk was designed around 1722 by James Gibbs for Sir Robert Walpole (1676–1745) and completed by Colen Campbell between

Dancing putti spreading garlands for a festivity, depicted in the stuccowork by Giuseppe Artari around the cornice of the Stone Hall at Houghton Hall, Norfolk

1723 and 1729. The austere Palladian exterior reveals interiors of a carefully calibrated progression of studied richness—permitted by rules of decorum within the Palladian canon. This is exemplified by an exterior of refined Palladian clarity, crowned by a statue of a Roman orator, and an interior with a stately but cool stone hall giving on to rooms of luxury and elegance, in which contrast of colour, texture, material, and tone was all-important. Thus a richness that equals the Baroque interior continues, but within a new sense of architectural discipline.

The interiors at Houghton Hall were largely designed by the architectural and furniture designer William Kent, himself one of the key players in the Palladian movement. Kent was an English painter trained in Rome who had come under the influence and patronage of Burlington, the leading champion of a new architecture sourced from the treatise of Andrea Palladio—which was in turn modelled on the treatise of Roman engineer Vitruvius in the fourth century A D.[2] Kent had been involved in decorative schemes elsewhere, including Kensington Palace, but Houghton is one of the first where he was clearly entrusted with the entire architectural and interior decoration of a major house. He could be considered one of the first interior decorators. Undoubtedly, Kent's particular talent was combining an enjoyable richness of interior with specific classical architectural detailing: pediments, columns, and architraves applied to doorcases and chimneypieces, with carefully proportioned cornices and ceiling compartments above.

The decoration at Houghton was inspired by the work of Palladio, by Kent's experiences in Rome, and by Palladio's early-seventeenth-century English

Houghton Hall as built for Sir Robert Walpole, 1st Earl of Orford, designed by James Gibbs, Colen Campbell, and William Kent

A group portrait showing
Sir Robert surrounded by
his family and friends in the
fashionable clothes worn in
these interiors. This painting,
by Charles Jervas and John
Wootton, hangs now in the
saloon at Houghton Hall.

champions Inigo Jones and John Webb, whose drawings had been collected by Lord Burlington. In 1774 John Vardy published *Some Designs of Mr Inigo Jones and Mr William Kent*, which included Kent's designs for Roman tables at Houghton.[3]

Houghton Hall's rooms of parade were designed by Kent for Sir Robert Walpole (later 1st Earl of Orford), who was then at the height of his power and prestige and the most powerful Whig politician in the land (he is regarded historically as in effect the first prime minster of England). Walpole was not from a great aristocratic dynasty, but from a Norfolk gentry family, and through ability achieved the highest political offices in the land. He regarded himself as a loyal servant to King George I.

Walpole intended Houghton to rival the great houses of the land, and the interiors were indeed regarded by one contemporary critic, Sir Thomas Robinson, as "a pattern for all great houses that may hereafter be built."[4] The interiors, where Walpole could entertain political allies (and potential allies), were largely finished by 1731, when the Duke of Lorraine was received there with lavish hospitality.

According to Lord Hervey, the "rustic story ... [was] dedicated to fox-hunters, hospitality, noise, dirt and business,"[5] while the first floor was described by another as "the floor of taste, expense, state and parade." The great rooms of parade on the first floor are in the Palladian manner and for great receptions would have been approached from the exterior stone steps. The internal staircase was painted in grisaille by Kent himself, vividly underlined in gilding. The principal panels show hunting scenes from the story

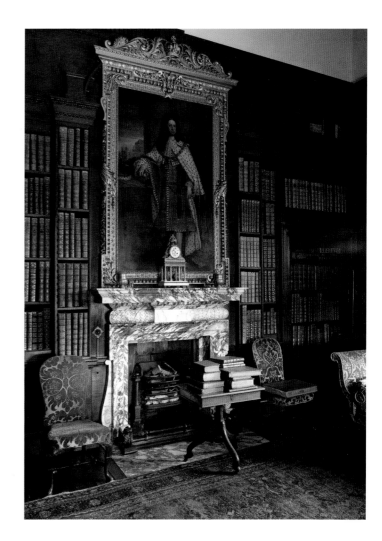

The early-eighteenth-century library designed by William Kent for Sir Robert Walpole, with Walpole's original desk and chair

of *Meleager and Atalanta*. The first-floor was divided between a suite of private rooms and a sequence of rooms of parade leading to a state apartment.

The private family rooms include the Common Parlour, where family members would sit, dine, read, and entertain close friends. Adjoining the Common Parlour, the library remains almost untouched today, a distinctly masculine room with classically detailed shelving suggesting Venetian windows. But while high-ceilinged and well-detailed, the family rooms have plain ceilings and are noticeably less ornate than the other rooms on the first floor.

At the heart of the house and a key room of parade on the *piano nobile* is the Stone Hall, a vast room with a balustraded gallery running around, a deliberate echo of the work of the early-seventeenth-century follower of Palladio, Inigo Jones, at the Queen's House at Greenwich and Whitehall. Although the colour of the walls and the plasterwork might well be described as cool, there is an almost overwhelming sense of richness and exuberance in the decorative detailing of the Stone Hall, especially the plasterwork ceiling by Italian stuccadore Giuseppe Artari.[6]

The core of the ceiling shows numerous putti playfully tugging at the garlands and dancing, as if preparing for a festivity. In the centre, the ribbon of the Order of the Garter, of which Walpole was the first commoner recipient, surrounds his coat of arms. The carved stone detailing around the two-stage chimneypieces and the doorcases, with triangular pediments supported by engaged columns, was designed by William Kent in the Palladian manner, following Inigo Jones's invention of Roman-inspired interior architecture. The sculptor Rysbrack carved the overmantel frieze depicting a sacrifice to Diana.

The bookcases were arranged to architectural effect around a Kentian chimneypiece in variegated marble.

overleaf *The magnificent ceiling of the Stone Hall, with stuccowork by Guiseppe Artari and the Walpole coat of arms in the centre. The pedimented doorcase leads into the saloon. The Stone Hall would also have served as a banqueting hall. The overmantel depicts a sacrifice to Diana, and the bust, sculpted by Rysbrack, shows Sir Robert in a Roman toga.*

*The saloon, inspired by
William Kent's knowledge of
Italian palazzo interiors*

Today the room is furnished almost exactly as it was in the early eighteenth century, with mahogany benches and handsomely carved mahogany side tables. Mahogany was in the 1720s a relatively new material for furnishing, and its import from the West Indies and South America was much encouraged by Robert Walpole himself. The consistency of Kent's design is shown in every detail, especially in the way that the benches are shaped to frame the scrolled brackets under which they sit.

The delicious contrast of the Palladian interior is perhaps felt most thrillingly in the movement between the cool, austere Stone Hall and the saloon, a large room for formal receptions that glows with crimson and gold.[7] The entrance to the room is through a pedimented doorcase. The hall's stone doorcase is in the Ionic order. The saloon's carved mahogany doorcase, in the Corinthian order, is picked out in oil gilding, as are all the window openings and other doorcases. For a moment on entry it is as if the architectural detailing of the Stone Hall had been projected into full-colour relief, the walls heavy with colour and gold, the architraves and chimneypiece also in carved mahogany with highlights in gilding.

The whole room is a brilliant evocation of the great *palazzi* that Kent knew from his time in Rome. The iconography of the plasterwork frieze and the ceiling painting by Kent also indicate a symbolic transition between the realm of Diana to that of Apollo (Diana and her hounds still appear in the richly gilded frieze). On the coved ceiling, roundels depict Neptune and Cybele for Water and Earth.

The ceiling painting depicts *Apollo Driving the Chariot of the Sun*, a popular

*The red caffoy is original,
as is the upholstery on the
Kent-designed chairs.*

subject encountered in other houses such as Boughton and Chatsworth. Kent may have derived this ceiling treatment from the ceiling in the Palazzo Barberini in Rome, which he had seen while training as a painter. Sir Robert Walpole insisted that the ceiling was painted in grisaille against a mosaic ground so that it would not overwhelm his picture collection below (the paintings, including works by Le Sueur, Snyders, Murillo, and Giordano, were sold after his death to the Empress Catherine the Great of Russia).[8]

The walls are still hung in the original crimson caffoy employed in the 1720s, a bolder and less refined material than the silk velvet that originally hung in the adjacent state rooms. The furniture is also that designed by Kent, and every item played its part in providing a consistent interior vision (as evidenced in Kent's surviving drawings). The pier glass frames, with unusually large mirror plates probably imported from France, and the pier tables below them were fully gilded and are typical of the solid magnificence of Kent's furniture designs, which were highly influential in the 1720s and '30s.

The rest of the original seat furniture of the room, which is still in situ today, is of carved and part-gilded mahogany, also a visual expression of the progress to be encountered in the succeeding state rooms, where the furniture would be fully gilded. The seat furniture was largely made on site by James Richards, the principal carver to the Office of Works and one of Kent's favourite craftsmen. It would normally be lined against the walls and brought out as needed.[9]

The White Drawing Room was originally hung in green velvet, green being the colour associated with Venus, the goddess of Love and Sleep, whose iconic shell motif is also depicted in the ceiling decoration. This room was rehung

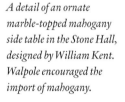

A detail of an ornate marble-topped mahogany side table in the Stone Hall, designed by William Kent. Walpole encouraged the import of mahogany.

The mahogany and part-gilded chairs in the saloon, probably made by James Richards, who was working at Houghton in 1726–29

*The Green Velvet
Bedchamber, with bed and
overmantel designed by
William Kent*

with brocaded silk hangings in the 1790s. The green is also found in the adjoining Green Velvet Bedchamber in the green velvet bed, designed with a huge shell (Venus's chariot) by Kent in a very architectural character.[10]

The bed survives in its original condition and position (the extravagance of the interior decoration and furnishing is illustrated by the survival of a 1732 bill for the trimmings of this bed for £1,219 3 s 11d). Venus also appears in the ceiling of the adjoining room (now the White Drawing Room).

The accompanying Brussels tapestries depict the story of *Venus and Vulcan* and *Venus and Adonis*. The ceiling painting shows *Aurora Rising*. The adjoining Tapestry Dressing Room was originally known as the Van Dyck Dressing Room and is still hung with tapestries depicting full-length portraits of the Stuart dynasty.

The Embroidered Bedchamber has a bed with embroidered hangings, worked in England but in the Indian style. This was the room used by the Duke of Lorraine on his visit in 1731. The Brussels tapestries here show tales of *Dionysus in Naxos* and *The Marriage of Dionysus to Ariadne*. The headboard and canopy both show Walpole's arms with the Order of the Garter. The vivid blue ceiling shows *Diana and Endymion* and other emblems of the night, including owls.

The adjoining room was originally an intimate picture cabinet in which Walpole had many of his finest paintings. It was originally hung with green silk velvet, as is shown by the surviving seat furniture (the chinoiserie theme was introduced after the sale of the pictures later in the eighteenth century). The seats, carved in mahogany, were upholstered in green velvet, and the chairs fully gilded in contrast to the part-gilding of the seat furniture in the Stone Hall.

opposite *A detail of the
green velvet bed, showing the
bedhead in the form of Venus's
attribute, the scallop shell. The
colour green was associated
with the goddess Venus.*

overleaf left *The Embroidered Bedchamber, with
bedhangings of Oriental-style
embroidery. The Brussels
tapestry scenes are from the
story of Dionysus.*

overleaf right *The cabinet
was originally hung in green
velvet, which survives on the
upholstered armchair.*

The Marble Parlour,
a marble-lined dining room
designed by William Kent,
with the buffet recesses from
where servants could serve
the meal

Another delicious contrast in colour and texture is the Marble Parlour, one of the earliest examples of a dining room designed as a part of a sequence of state rooms.[11] Here the decoration was an innovation suggested by James Gibbs, the marble-lined walls perhaps inspired by the state rooms at Versailles. Previously, dining was much more of a mobile affair, with tables set up in different rooms, including the Stone Hall, which was a symbolic and practical banqueting hall. The Victoria and Albert Museum now owns and advises on the conservation of the elaborate beds and seat furniture.

Creating a permanent dining room was an opportunity to create a temple to Bacchus, the god of wine. The ornate ceiling is decorated with dense bunches of grapes in green, gold, and ochre. The marble side tables recessed behind a marble buffet screen would have been for the display of silver gilt plate.

The overmantel shows a *Sacrifice to Bacchus* carved by Rysbrack (who probably advised on the selection of marble), and the pedimented and lobed frame is typical of William Kent. The cumulative visual effect of the variegated marbles and the gilding and painted decoration creates a breathtaking ensemble. The arched recesses were designed to give servants a point to enter the room to serve and to offer warming spaces for food behind the chimneypiece.

Houghton Hall illustrates as well as any of the great houses of the period the continuing brilliant theatre of the country house interior, the dramatic difference between the rooms for private family occupation and those designed for the reception of honoured guests, the rooms of parade, and the layered and contrasting moods of the state rooms, with their increasing costliness of materials and brilliance of gilding.

The survival of so much original detail and furniture, despite inevitable changes over three centuries (including the loss of the major picture collection), allows us to feel something of the visual culture of Walpole and his contemporaries. Thanks to the present Marquis of Cholmondley, advice from the late John Cornforth, and experts from the Victoria and Albert Museum, the rooms are presented in a way that helps us feel the degree of ornate luxury in the Palladian country house, with its evocation of the classical world and the admired *palazzi* of Rome and Venice.[12] Kent had a painterly sense of the unity of architecture, ornament, and furnishing, and clearly both he and his patron, Walpole, revelled in the subtleties of classical and Palladian motif, and in the overt and veiled iconography expressed in painted and carved form.

7 HOLKHAM HALL

The Palladian Interior II

HOLKHAM HALL IN NORFOLK IS ONE OF ENGLAND'S NEO-PALLADIAN paradigms, a great house designed in the spirit of a classical Roman villa and informed by the work of sixteenth-century Italian architect Andrea Palladio. It was built for Thomas Coke (1697–1759), who spent nearly six years on the Grand Tour (1712–18), and met Lord Burlington's protégé, William Kent, in Rome. Returning in 1718, he married Lady Margaret Tufton, a daughter of the 1st Earl of Thanet, plunged into a political career as a Whig, and began planning his new house in Norfolk, which was not completed until 1765, six years after his death. His widow brought the work to completion "to commemorate

A detail of the warm-coloured variegated alabaster of the Marble Hall at Holkham Hall, Norfolk

in the most perfect manner the Taste, the Elegance and the refined erudition of its illustrious founder."[1]

Thomas Coke, created Viscount Lovell in 1728 and in 1744, the 1st Earl of Leicester (of the fifth creation), took the greatest interest in the building project and is regarded by some scholars as in effect the architect of his own house, although he was certainly also advised by Lord Burlington and William Kent, and had the services of a highly competent executant architect, Matthew Brettingham. Among Coke's letters to Matthew Brettingham, Sr., is one that refers to the design of Holkham being approved by Burlington: "It is w[i]th pleasure I can inform you our whole design is vastly approved of by Ld. Burlington, he says the insides plan the best he ever saw. Kents outside is also vastly in favour & the going up steps from the hall also."[2]

The main house of parade was arranged around two courtyards, while four matching pavilions furnished the family's private apartments and library; the guest wing (known then as now as the Stranger's Wing); the chapel; and the kitchen and other rooms for servants. The main rooms were designed around the display of art. Coke had collected sculptures, books, manuscripts, and paintings on his Grand Tour (writing while travelling "I am become since my stay in Rome, a perfect virtuoso, and a great lover of pictures").[3] He had also studied architectural drawings and design in Rome with architect Giacomo Mariari. Coke's vision was a huge house with a central palatial block with rooms appropriate for the display of his treasures—a built expression of his erudite knowledge of classical literature and mythology full of deliberate visual allusions, not just in iconographic terms but also in architectural reference.

His house was to be a rustic villa "worthy of the ancients." Kent's interior drew heavily on the example of the celebrated Inigo Jones, who, as we saw with his work at Wilton, had invented the necessary detail for the architectural Palladian interior, and whose designs for chimneypieces and doorcases were engraved and published by Kent while he was working on Houghton and Holkham in 1727. Coke's building project was severely delayed because he

overleaf *Fluted Ionic columns modelled on the example of the Temple of Fortuna Virilis in Rome*

lost money in the South Sea Bubble disaster. Work finally began in 1734, and yellow brick was chosen over stone for the external structure. Nonetheless the result was a triumph, and Arthur Young writing in the 1770s observed that it was perhaps the best of all the great houses of its generation, "so convenient a house does not exist—so admirably adapted to the *English* way of living, and so ready to be applied to the grand or the comfortable stile of life."[4]

Coke demonstrated his knowledge and understanding of the classical world not just in objects, books, and conversation (there are descriptions of him and his friends hunting fox all day and spending the evenings discussing classical literature), but also in the designs for Holkham. This is illustrated in the entrance hall, known as the Marble Hall, a glorious banqueting hall hinting at the account of the banquet of the gods described in Ovid's *Metamorphoses*—the source for so much of the iconography of ornamental detail in this period.[5]

The hall must rank as one of the most unforgettable rooms in Europe, and into it Coke poured his experience and imagination. When the plans and elevations were published in 1773, the younger Brettingham (who helped publish the designs) wrote: "The idea of the Great Hall was suggested by the Earl himself, from the judicious and learned Palladio's example of a Basilica or tribunal justice, exhibited in his Designs for Monsignor Barbaro's translation of Vitruvius."[6] The reference to justice was a nod to Coke's descent from the famous Elizabethan law giver.

The interior decoration was derived from both architectural and ornamental detail. A colonnade that runs around at first-floor gallery level was modelled on the Temple of Fortuna Virilis in Rome (sourced from Antoine Desgodetz's 1682 *Les édifices antiques de Rome*), and the fifty-foot-high coffered ceiling was based on the example of the famous Pantheon temple, also in Rome. The arrangement of the choir of Palladio's Redentore Church has also been suggested as a model for the apsidal arrangement of the hall, which may also have been influenced by the character of the contemporary opera stage, given Coke's love of Italian opera.

In 1726 the contemporary architect Giacomo Leoni published a translation of Leon Battista Alberti's *Ten Books*, in which Alberti describes an entrance hall as a kind of personal temple: "exactly answering the middle of your Courtyard place your entrance, with a handsome vestibule… Let the first room that offers itself be a chapel dedicated to God; with its Altar, where Strangers and Guests may offer their devotions, beginning their Friendship by Religion; and where the Father of the family may put up his prayers for the peace of his house and the welfare of his relations."[7] Some scholars go further and suggest that the model for this great room could be the Temple of Solomon (Coke was also a leading Freemason).

Rich colour is expressed in the materials themselves. The warmth of the Derbyshire alabaster columns is a brilliant innovation, and the deeply coffered and gilded plasterwork and mahogany doors contribute further depth and texture to the whole. The alabaster detail was carved by masons on site. The niches are still filled today with plaster copies of classical Greek and Roman statues. Designs by Kent survive to show that his original concept for the hall was modified in execution, the design of the original concave staircase intended to frame a statue of Jupiter.

The cool feeling of imperial authority and power expressed in the Marble Hall is in delicious and deliberate contrast to the saloon at the top of the stone

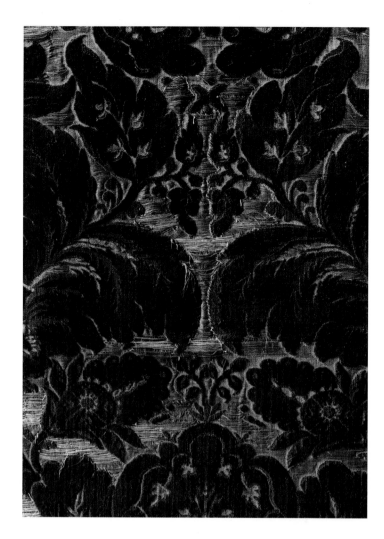

steps. As at Houghton, the saloon was (and is still) hung in crimson caffoy, a mixture of silk, linen, and wool. The choice of Sicilian jasper for the two chimneypieces in this room emphasised the warmth of the colour scheme. The coved ceiling is coffered and part gilded, and is based on a ceiling from the Roman Basilica of Maxentius, the panels filled with gilded sunflowers sacred to Apollo.[8]

This splendid room retains its original furniture, including narrow gilt pier tables with two oval pier glasses, one above the other, which reflected candle-light. The two larger sideboard tables incorporate mosaic pavement reputed to have been excavated from the Villa Adriana, the residence of the Emperor Hadrian. Bought from the Cardinal Furietti, the mosaic fragments were famous and prized objects of antiquity. For these precious and illustrious objects, supports of extraordinary lightness were designed, the legs formed by depictions of ostriches with outstretched wings, an allusion to the ostriches in the Coke coat of arms.[9] The tall arched windows of the south wall give onto the vast Corinthian portico, the central feature of the south front of Holkham that feels like a temple-fronted loggia looking over the park.

To the west of the saloon lies the drawing room, also richly decorated with walls hung in "crimson flowered Genoa Velvet." This also gave access to the Statue Gallery—one of the most important in an English country house as the first to be solely dedicated to the display of sculpture. Its design may have been influenced by Scamozzi's reconstruction of the main building of the Roman House, with a central room between two tribunes. The gallery was filled with sculptures collected mostly in 1716–17 while on his Grand Tour and include

right A detail of a chair and side table supported by carved and gilded ostriches. Mosaic fragments set in marble were excavated from Hadrian's villa near Rome.

The Statue Gallery, one of the few surviving purpose-built sculpture galleries of the eighteenth century to display its original collection. The seat furniture has been reupholstered with the original blue leather.

some that were considered the finest classical sculptures in an English collection, especially the statue of Diana over the chimneypiece (which also bears on the frieze a head of Apollo), the statues of Neptune, and that of Marsyas, as well as statues of ancient philosophers. It has been suggested that the entire arrangement of the gallery was a kind of celebration of the pastoral idyll celebrated in Virgil's *Eclogues*. The glories of this gallery can be read as a statement about Coke's transformation of the barren wastelands around the house into a productive estate, crowned with this celebration of civilisation, the house itself as alluded to in the inscription in the hall raised by his widow.

The Statue Gallery was described warmly in 1752 by a visitor, the Admiral Boscawen, as a "Chambre d'Assembly, elegant to a degree."[10] He also commented on how it looked when lit up especially. The North Tribune linked the gallery to the North Dining Room, which was also dedicated to classical sculpture. The huge apse, in which a sideboard table stood, was modelled on a detail from Desgodetz, and a ceiling after a design by Inigo Jones. The tablet

set in the chimneypiece shows an event from Aesop's *Fables*. Much of the icon-ographical detail refers to Bacchus and Ceres, for wine and food.

To the east of the saloon lie the rooms of display associated with a late-seventeenth- and early-eighteenth-century house, the Grand Apartment: in effect, a drawing room (now the south dining room), dressing room, and state bedchamber. The state dressing room, long known as the Landscape Room, doubled as a picture cabinet and is hung densely, as it was in the eighteenth century. The pictures are principally landscapes collected by Coke on his Grand Tour, including seven by Claude Lorrain and others by Poussin, Lucatelli, and Vernet. One door leads to the gallery for the private chapel; the other door leads to the Green State Bedroom.

This was the visual highpoint of the Great Apartment. The great bed, "a flowered Genoa Velvet Bed, of three colours," was designed en suite with the pelmets and curtains, and all the upholstered furniture was designed by William Kent.[11] The bedroom's decoration in marble, textiles, paint, and

A view from the North Tribune to the Marble Hall, with sculptures of Juno and Lucius Antonius on either side

*The Landscape Room,
originally the state dressing
room, hung with paintings
collected by the 1st Earl on his
Grand Tour*

plasterwork created a rich, jewel-like interior, full of floral imagery—the latter alluding to the Roman ideal of a Golden Age, everlasting spring, and eternal youth. The tapestries on either side of the chimneypiece, representing America and Africa, are by Flemish weaver Albert Auwercx. The three other tapestries, designed by Francesco Zuccarelli, were woven by Paul Saunders in Soho. One represents Asia, but those on either side of the bed represented Sleep and Vigilance. Zuccarelli painted the overdoor pictures representing the Four Seasons. The painting over the chimneypiece shows the God Jupiter caressing his wife, Juno.

The north front had a corresponding state apartment, approached from the Marble Hall through the north state drawing room, hung with four large Brussels tapestries, probably woven by Gerland Peemans in the late seventeenth century. The gilt seat furniture, upholstered in crimson, was designed by William Kent. The north state bedchamber was also hung with tapestry and had a mosaic slab from a Roman villa and other "curious antique mosaic for Adrian's villa."[12] The tablet in the chimneypiece shows the *Birth of the Poet*, after Montfaucon, *L'Antiquité Expliquée* (1719–24), another popular source.

John Cornforth remarked how Holkham "remains a complete work of art, with a strong intellectual purpose."[13] The atmospheric resonance of the rooms of parade owes much to the recent programme of conservation and redisplay carried out by the Earl and Countess of Leicester and continued by Lord Leicester's son, Viscount Coke, who took over the home in 2009.[14]

*Provided by Paul Saunders
of Soho after a design by
Zuccarelli, a detail of the
tapestry depicting Sleep in the
Green State Bedroom*

*The magnificent state
bed in the Green State
Bedroom designed by
William Kent and
upholstered in a very
expensive three-coloured
cut velvet, also used
for the curtains and
armchair upholstery*

8 HAREWOOD
HOUSE

The Genius of Robert Adam I

HAREWOOD HOUSE IN YORKSHIRE IS A HOUSE OF MANY LAYERS. IT was designed by John Carr of York and begun in 1759, while the interiors were mostly designed by Scottish-born Robert Adam (1728–1792). In the 1840s the house was altered by Sir Charles Barry (Herbert Baker also worked here in the 1930s for the Princess Royal). The Lascelles were an old Yorkshire family who had made their fortune in the sugar trade in Barbados, and the building and decoration of Harewood House was part of their economic ascendancy that led them to become Earls of Harewood by the end of the eighteenth century. Henry Lascelles (d.1753) had acquired the manors of Harewood and

A detail of the ceiling of the library at Harewood House (originally the saloon), with the characteristic neoclassical detail championed by Robert Adam

Gawthorpe in the 1750s for £68, 828. He then divided his fortune—derived from his plantations and his role as collector of customs for Bridgetown in Barbados—between his two sons: Edwin (an MP who became 1st Baron Harewood, builder of Harewood House), and his brother Daniel, who was head of the plantation businesses until his death in 1784. After Daniel's death, Edwin inherited all the estates and continued to add to their working plantations.[1]

Edwin Lascelles met Robert Adam in 1758, when the cultivated and ambitious young architect had just returned from his Italian Grand Tour. Lascelles had already had designs for his new house drawn up by the highly competent, York-based Palladian architect John Carr. Perhaps surprisingly, Lascelles asked Adam to see what could be done to improve the designs, and to add fresh neoclassical taste.

Carr's reaction is not recorded. It is known that Lascelles also showed the suggestions to the 1st Earl of Leicester, the builder of Holkham, whom he regarded as his architecture guru. James Adam mentioned in one letter that his brother Robert had "tickled up" Carr's designs to "dazzle the Eyes of the squire."[2] Relatively little of Adam's advice, intended to bring more movement and variety into the elevation and plans, was actually taken onboard by Carr. However, Adam was clearly given a leading hand with the interiors, based on the example of architecture and decoration discovered in recent excavations in Italy, and most of his designs and plans are preserved at the Sir John Soane's Museum in London.

Even though Adam's commission was principally for interior work, Harewood ranks as one of his largest country house projects, with a total of

The south front of Harewood House, Yorkshire. Designed by John Carr of York, with interiors by Robert Adam, the house was adapted by Sir Charles Barry in the early nineteenth century.

right *The extraordinary range of furniture supplied to Harewood House by Thomas Chippendale includes (clockwise from top left) the neoclassical sideboard, the green lacquered clothespress, a chair in the music room, and the Diana and Minerva commode.*

some seventeen rooms decorated between 1765 and 1771. During this period, Adam was quickly emerging as one of the leading neoclassical architects of his generation. He revelled in plasterwork and painted decoration, which he described as "all delicacy, gaiety and beauty."

Edwin Lascelles combined an obvious ambition with a sense of caution; he wrote to Adam directly about his projected level of expenditure: "I would not exceed the limits of expense that I have always set myself. Let us do everything properly and well, mais pas trop."[3] Lascelles's largesse, however, made it possible for Adam to fulfil one of his finest sequences of interiors. The effect of these great rooms owed much, both then and now, to the remarkable sequence of furniture at Harewood that was supplied by the master cabinetmaker Thomas Chippendale (1718–1779) and his son, also Thomas.

Chippendale worked on Harewood alongside Adam from 1767. Although born in Yorkshire, Chippendale was by then based on St. Martin's Lane in London and was well established on a trajectory that would make him one of the most famous furniture makers in England. Like the Adam brothers, he made himself a household name by publishing his designs, and his *Gentleman and Cabinet-makers' Director* (1754–62) inevitably encouraged imitators as much as it attracted clients. Adam did not design the furniture here, as he did elsewhere, but had confidence in Chippendale's ability, and indeed Chippendale visited the rooms to study the ornament and see how his furniture could reflect Adam's work. One contemporary visitor wrote of his furniture "having great affinity with the Stucco and Carved Ornament in each apartment."[4]

The range of Chippendale's work at Harewood is staggering, from the green and gold lacquer furniture now shown in the East Bedroom, to the exquisite seat furniture in a French style in the music room, everything designed with a sense of glamour but also with decorum and appropriateness to each room. (There are some fifteen different designs for chairs alone, supplied by Chippendale for this house.)[5]

The mid- to late-eighteenth century is the first great age of the cabinetmaker (other leading figures include Vile and Cobb, Ince and Mayhew, Matthew Hallett, and the Linnells), but in few other country houses in England do we see this as clearly as we do at Harewood.[6] Furniture was supplied by Chippendale's firm from 1767 until 1797, by which time Thomas Chippendale Sr. had died and his son was directing the business (he especially completed the work to the White Drawing Room and the picture gallery). It is thought that over £10,000 was spent on the furniture for Harewood alone, many times what other great landowners paid Chippendale (the house itself cost around £30,000 to build).

The marble-floored entrance hall created an atrium to the great state apartments beyond and may have been inspired in part by the hall at Wentworth Woodhouse, where Carr had worked in the 1760s. In decorative terms it combines the trademark Adam touches intended to add boldness and movement to Carr's original proposals: the walls are divided by engaged Doric columns and niches for sculpture, which create the stately rhythm of a triumphal arch, especially around the main entrance to the saloon, where the doorcase sits within a relieving arch. Also, the elegant plasterwork ceiling is divided into symmetrical and geometrical compartments framing medallions drawn from known classical sources.

The plaster roundels above the chimneypieces have trophies of arms

overleaf *The entrance hall is a typical example of Robert Adam's unified interiors with engaged columns, running Greek frieze, and plasterwork ceiling. William Collins's chimneypiece panel shows the wedding of Neptune and Amphitrite. The hall chairs are by Thomas Chippendale. The porphyry colour of the columns derives from a scheme later than Adam's.*

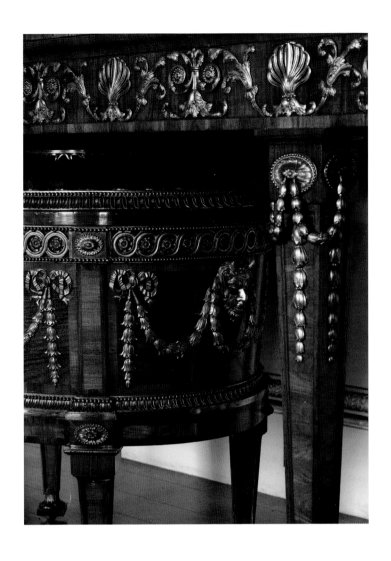

*A detail of the marble
chimneypiece and
overmantel relief painting
by Biagio Rebecca*

echoing the triumphal theme, while the main overmantel carved by William Collins shows *The Marriage of Neptune and Amphitrite*. On the corresponding west wall, another relief by Collins depicts the *Chariot of Phaeton* (the original chimneypiece on this wall was later removed). The carved and painted beechwood hall chairs are those supplied by Chippendale.

It is interesting to compare the heroic style of the hall, originally "stony white"[7] to the more delicate scheme of the Old Library, the first room to the east of the hall, which has been repainted in its original colour scheme of grey, green, and white. The library originally served as the private family drawing room and is comfortable and elegant. The painted panels in the library depicting mythological scenes are by Biagio Rebecca, and are set above the chimneypiece and above alternating bookcases, with busts in between. As in the entrance hall, the walls are broken up with pilasters and arches above the other bookcases. Chippendale supplied the chairs and the expandable library steps in rosewood with exotic inlaid decoration and ormolu ornament.

The room at the centre of all the great rooms of the south front was the saloon, now called the library. This would have been approached directly from the cool entrance hall. The visitor would have felt the same degree of contrast between an almost exterior space to the first grand and imposing room of reception, as at Houghton Hall and Holkham Hall. The full effect of Adam's original design here was different from that experienced today, as the room was fitted up into an elegant library by Charles Barry in the 1840s, with shelves curving into Adam's apsidal recesses. Barry did leave Adam's original decorated semi-domed ceilings of these apses intact. The apses were cleverly designed to reflect the tall, gilt-framed pier glasses between the windows of the south wall. The two elegant pedimented chimneypieces were carved for the saloon by John Deval and frame circular reliefs by William Collins, originally bronzed. The ceiling has the typically delicate and refined plasterwork of Adam's designs, with repeated urns and rosettes, framed by swags and borders

*A detail of the centre of the
ceiling of the Old Library*

right *The Old Library
was designed as the private
family drawing room off the
entrance hall. The original
grey, green, and white colour
scheme has been restored. The
chairs are all by Chippendale.*

overleaf *The state
bedchamber. The green silk
damask on the bed and
walls was rewoven as part
of a major restoration in
1999–2000. The Diana and
Minerva commode, top left,
made by Thomas Chippendale
in 1773, is one of his best-
known pieces of furniture.*

with a running Greek key pattern, executed by Joseph Rose, Adam's favourite stuccoist. Rose worked on all the plaster ceilings of the house.[8]

The long sequence of grand rooms to the south was divided into two parts. To the east of the saloon lies the Great Apartment, the state dressing room (now known as the Spanish Library) with an original Adam ceiling, and the state bedroom; while on the west lay two drawing rooms leading to the gallery on the west front, the dining room, and the music room on the north front.

The state bedchamber is an extraordinary sight. Since the recent restoration of the glorious state bed, which had been dismantled in the 1840s, one feels the sheer bravura of interior decoration as expressed in the architecture of Adam and the furnishings of Chippendale. The ornate plasterwork ceiling is reflected in the great gilded canopy of Chippendale's expertly restored state bed, hung with its shimmering green silk damask, rewoven in 1999 to match the original pattern and trimmed lavishly with expensive fringe and elaborate tassels. The bed was described in the bill as "Gilt in Burnished Gold" and is in some ways more like a garden temple than a traditional Baroque state bed.[9]

The bed was designed to stand in a niche between Ionic columns, *à la française*. The original niche was deeper, but during the early-nineteenth-century alterations it was reduced to provide a corridor behind. The original furnishings for the room also included the Chippendale-designed gilt-framed mirrors and the black and gold Oriental lacquer cabinets, providing yet another contrast of colour and texture that contributed to the overall richness of the scene. The magnificent inlaid Diana and Minerva commode is shown in this room today.

To the west of the saloon lay two large rooms of reception, the Yellow Drawing Room and the White Drawing Room, which lead to the huge picture gallery that runs the full depth of the house at its west end. Initially called the drawing room, the Yellow Drawing Room was rehung with yellow silk from 1776 and furnished with yellow and silver furniture by Chippendale, as well as a pier glass, chimney glass, and a pair of mirrored girandoles, all "highly finished in Burnished silver."[10] For the ceiling Adam adapted the pattern of an antique Roman example engraved by Pietro Santi Bartoli, the late-seventeenth-century artist and draughtsman who engraved and published many of the great antiquities of Rome (a new edition of Bartoli's *Antichi Sepolchri* was published in 1768). The original colour scheme was of pink and green on the ceiling with yellow silk on the walls.

The next drawing room was described on earlier plans as the south dining room but was actually finished as a drawing room. In the 1780s the room was completed with white silk damask bordered with gold and "seven elegant glasses ornamented with festoons, particularily light and beautiful, also tables with the same." It then became known as the White Drawing Room. The white damask was replaced in more recent years with a cinnamon-coloured silk as a suitable background to eighteenth-century family portraits. Additional decorative paintings were added to the ceiling by Alfred Stevens in 1852.[11]

The west front of the house is filled with the vast gallery, measuring seventy-six feet, ten inches by twenty-four feet, three inches—a "Great Room of Entertainment" as well as a place to display treasures. This impressive room took a considerable amount of time to refine. The ceiling was designed in 1769, but it took some years for Lascelles to agree to the designs for the monumental chimneypiece opposite the central Venetian window of the outside wall.[12]

The Yellow Drawing Room was hung with yellow silk in 1776. The overmantel is by Chippendale.

The ceiling of the 1770s gallery is filled with painted panels by Biagio Rebecca.

The wall on which the picture collection is displayed is reflected in the tall pier glasses and marble-topped pier tables and gilded torchères on the window wall. The piers between windows are actually the darkest spots in the room and a better place for mirrors than paintings. The Venetian windows at either end are formed with *verde antico* columns, and all the windows are crowned with gilded pelmets to which appear to be gathered the most remarkable richly festooned curtains (they are in fact rendered in carved and painted wood). The adjoining dining room was remodelled by Barry in the 1840s but still retains Chippendale's sideboard tables, wine cooler, and urn-topped pedestals.

Best preserved of all the interiors is probably the music room.[13] A brilliant sense of drama is created by the large-scale paintings of classical ruins by Antonio Zucchi, which would have amused an eighteenth-century visitor as contrasting the revived Rome of Adam's new architecture. Musical themes in roundels are arranged in the ceiling based on the example of a painted vault in the Palace of Augustus in Rome (as published by Bernard de Montfaucon, from the *Supplément au livre de l'antiquité expliquée*, 1724, one of the key sources

The festooned curtains are actually carved in wood and painted and were supplied by Chippendale the Younger.

left and above *The music room is dominated by four pictures by Antonio Zucchi depicting great Roman ruins. The seat furniture was originally supplied by Chippendale for the state bed and dressing rooms. The carpet reflects Adam's ceiling design, and the overmantel frame is by Chippendale.*

for such designs). The ceiling roundels depict Apollo and the nine muses with Minerva, with *Apollo Victorious in the Music Contest with Marsyas, Judged by King Midas* in the centre. The pattern of the ceiling is vividly echoed in the pattern of the Axminster carpet. A lyre appears in the carved marble chimneypiece. The elegant chairs and sofas now in this room were all designed by Chippendale but were originally found in the state bedroom and dressing room.[14]

Despite the layers added by Barry and Baker in later works, we are still privileged to see much of the quality of Adam's and Chippendale's work, so wonderfully preserved and presented today by the Earl and Countess of Harewood and their dedicated team of curators. One eighteenth-century visitor called Forrest wrote that Harewood House was "one of the best and compleatest Houses in the Kingdom, where elegance and Convenience are so Happily united."

A detail of a muse from the ceiling roundels

9 SYON HOUSE

The Genius of Robert Adam II

SYON HOUSE IN MIDDLESEX IS ONE OF THE HISTORIC POSSESSIONS of the Percy family. Its plan is based on that of the former monastic house, altered for the family in the late sixteenth century. The interiors of the house, however, were utterly transformed in the 1760s by Robert Adam for Hugh Smithson (1714–1786), 1st Earl of Northumberland (created 1st Duke in 1766), and his countess, Elizabeth Percy, a descendant of the Percy Earls of Northumberland and heiress of some of their great estates. Smithson changed his name to Percy in deference.[1]

Syon House was among a sequence of great country houses and town houses

A detail of the ceiling of the Red Drawing Room: the design was probably inspired by that of the Villa Madama in Rome. Cipriani painted 239 medallions depicting classical subjects.

Syon House as seen from the approach. Originally a monastic house, it was rebuilt in the sixteenth century, and the interior was entirely transformed by Robert Adam in the 1760s. The exterior was refaced in Bath Stone in the 1820s.

whose interiors Adam built or remodelled during the 1760s and 1770s, making him one of the two most influential architects of those decades, alongside Sir William Chambers, who had also trained in Rome and with whom he shared the role of Architect of the King's Works. The Duke was considered an important patron of the arts, to whom Chippendale dedicated his *Director*. In a masterstroke of publicity and self-promotion that inspired many imitators of his style, Adam published the designs of these houses during the 1770s with his brother James.[2]

These engravings celebrated "the novelty and variety" of their designs as the brothers argued, "we have not trod in the path of others, nor derived aid from their labours" but prided themselves on having introduced "a great diversity of ceilings, friezes and decorated pilasters, and to have added grace and beauty to the whole, by a mixture of grotesque stucco, painted ornaments, together with flowing *rainceau* [decorative friezes]."[3] Robert Adam's introduction of decoration with tablets and medallions into ceilings, walls, and furniture, as well as in the use of low-relief stuccowork, earned him the nickname "Bob the Roman." He was the champion of a new generation's pursuit of the antique, which supplanted Palladianism and has become known, in modern times, as neoclassicism (here seen in its earliest phase before designers embraced the model of ancient Greece).

Clearly Robert Adam was an ambitious architect with a vision of the transforming possibilities of interior decoration following classical Roman models, which could also supply "variety and amusement" to his clients. At Syon House, Adam responded to his commission with one of the most

overleaf Two views of the Great Hall, a vast room modelled by Robert Adam on a Roman basilica and inspired by the work of Piranesi. At each end the view is framed by a fine piece of classical sculpture: a plaster copy of the Apollo Belvedere *and a bronze version by Valadier of* The Dying Gaul *from the Capitoline Museum in Rome.*

right *The breathtaking splendour of the anteroom with ceiling and trophy panels by Joseph Rose, and the gilded figures of gods and goddesses. The columns, veneered in verde antico scagliola, were acquired as Roman originals, which had reputedly been brought up from the bed of the Tiber in 1762.*

full-blooded of the neoclassical interiors of the period, which owed much to his obvious rapport with the Duke. The interiors have architectural grandeur and yet in parts also have a lightness and decorative quality that is still associated with the name Adam. His palette is also immediately recognisable: pale greens, pink, and blues as background, relieved by inset paintings or delicate plasterwork.

The interiors at Syon House are in a spirit that Adam had learned so well during his extended four-year Grand Tour of Italy and his association with antiquary and author Piranesi. He had also taken intensive tours of the surviving remains of classical antiquity alongside the French artist Clérisseau, who tutored him and helped form his taste for antique architecture and ornament.

Adam was hired by the 1st Duke in 1761; Adam had returned from Italy in 1758, so his travels were still fresh in his mind. The extraordinarily stately sequence of rooms contrived at Syon House was realised by the finest craftsmen of the day, Italians and Englishmen: Joseph Rose the stuccoist, sculptors John Wilton and John Cheere, decorative painters Michelangelo Pergolesi and Pietro Cipriani, and figurative painters Francesco Zuccarelli and Andrea Casali.

At Syon House, Adam felt he had achieved a building "in a magnificent manner … entirely in the Antique Style" and paid homage to his patron "who possessed not only wealth to execute a great design but skill to judge of its merit."[4] The 1st Duke was well travelled and from 1770 was also working with Adam at Northumberland House (which was demolished in 1874, although elements of the celebrated glass drawing room can be seen in the Victoria and Albert Museum).

The Adam rooms begin with the Great Hall, modelled on a classical Roman basilica and completed in 1769. When Robert Adam and his brother James published *Works in Architecture*, they wrote that the hall at Syon House was "a room of great dimension and finished in stucco" and pointed out how the different recesses at either end gave a "noble effect and increased the variety." The hall was conceived as a classical banqueting hall, its decoration evoking the Arch of Constantine, including its Hadrianic reliefs.[5]

The room was also furnished with ancient classical sculpture, acquired by Robert's brother James and displayed upon pedestals designed by Robert Adam, as well as busts of philosophers and emperors. At one end a coffered apse frames a figure of the Apollo Belvedere (a copy by John Cheere of the admired sculpture in the Vatican collection). It was originally intended to house the Laocoön Group. At the other end of the room, a screen of enriched Doric columns frames the bronze sculpture of a dying gladiator by Luigi Valadier. The whole ensemble is grand and cool, but the diversity of shapes allows for an extraordinary play of light and shadow.

The most astonishing neoclassical room in England must be the anteroom, which illustrates most vividly the neoclassical designers' desire to create a living version of Greek and Roman architecture. The details based on Greek and Roman prototypes were probably sourced in the engravings and work of author of antiquary Piranesi, who was such an important influence on Adam and his generation. The anteroom was ornamented in "splendid manner" and "decorated with columns of verd antique marble," which were reputedly ancient columns raised from the bed of the Tiber, finished in a green scagliola with gilded capitals for reuse here.[6]

overleaf The dining room, completed by Adam in 1763, with apsidal ends screened by Corinthian columns. The niches facing the window wall frame gods and goddesses, such as Bacchus and Ceres. The porphyry painted backgrounds were most likely part of a later Regency scheme.

The ceiling plasterwork was inspired by the Villa Madama in Rome: the
pattern of the ceiling (published in *Works in Architecture*) is reflected in the
colours of the highly polished scagliola floor. Rose also produced the gilded
trophy panels, which are derived from those ancient Roman examples found
on the Capitoline, which Adam knew from his time in Rome. Gilded statues of
the loving deities, gods, and goddesses taken from Piranesi's works crowned
the screens of columns. The statuary marble chimneypiece is enhanced by
sculpted Bacchic rams' heads, above which is a plaque after the antique of a
subject known as *The Roman Bride*. The gilt tables have marble tops, which were
also acquired in Rome. The colourful floor was substantially but faithfully
renewed in the early nineteenth century.

The screen of columns that faced the entrance hall helped give the
impression of a square-shaped room and also mediated the turn towards the
succeeding Great Apartment. Here Adam sought to combine the "variety and
gracefulness of form, so particularly courted by the ancients," with the "proper
arrangement and relief of apartments … in which the French have excelled all
other nations; these have united magnificence with utility."

The first room is the state dining room, a long room with a series of three
niches on each side of the chimneypiece framing classical sculpture, including
a copy of Michelangelo's *Bacchus*, carved by Joseph Wilton for the 1st Duke.
Also here is sculpture acquired in Rome by James Adam, including a version
of the Farnese Flora by the then famous sculptor Cavaceppi. These niches face
the window wall, which is further lightened by the presence of gilt pier glasses
between the windows.

The chimneypiece was carved by Thomas and Benjamin Carter to Adam's designs. The overmantel relief depicts *The Three Graces*, the daughters of Zeus, by Luc-François Breton, for which the Duke paid £70. On either side of the chimneypiece are grisaille paintings suggesting carved relief, painted by Andrea Casali, one showing a famous scene of an ancient Roman fresco, known as the Aldobrandini wedding. Adam designed the pier glasses and tables, and the overall colour scheme was originally more consistent, described by a contemporary as "all elegant & white & gold."[7] The 1st Duke and his Duchess are depicted in relief portraits in the plasterwork.

Adam famously remarked how important the dining room was to the English, who "indulge most largely in the enjoyment of the bottle. Every person of rank here is either a member of the legislation, or entitled by his condition to take part in the political arrangements of his country, or to enter with ardour into those discussions to which they give rise."[8] So Englishmen spend more time here than their French counterparts and "Instead of being hung with damask, tapestry, &c, [dining rooms] are always finished with stucco, and adorned with statues and paintings, that they may not retain the smell of the victuals."

The next room is the superbly palatial state drawing room, which Adam compared to the French *salle de compagnie*, hung with a rich, three-coloured damask (reversed when rehung in 1965). The ceiling "coved and painted in compartments" is another of Adam's *coups de theatre* at Syon House. Many variant designs survive for this ceiling, for which the final version is a compact, mosaic pattern of octagons, diamonds, and roundels.

The Red Drawing Room, with its magnificent ceiling and finely detailed chimneypiece. The walls are hung in crimson damask, which was reversed in the 1960s to give it a longer life, and the carpet is an original designed by Adam and made by Thomas Moore of Moorfields in London in 1769.

The subjects of the 239 roundels, painted on paper by Cipriani, seem to have been chosen by the Duke himself from the engraved illustrations in Montfaucon's *Antiquity Explained* (first published in the 1720s), based on the pictures uncovered in ancient Roman houses at Herculaneum and also from Grecian elements taken from Lysicrates illustrated by James Stuart in his 1762 *Antiquities of Athens*. Diarist and historian James Lee-Milne wrote that he thought that they looked like "skied dinner plates."[9] Also in this room are two pier tables made up to Adam's design for "two noble pieces of antique mosaic found in Titus's baths."[10] The original carpet was also designed by Adam and woven by Thomas Moore of Moorefields in 1769 with a Greek honeysuckle pattern repeated in the ceiling. The two doorcases were decorated in ormolu displayed against an ivory background.

The old Jacobean Long Gallery was transformed into an enormously long and elegant living room—considered apparently a suitable retiring room for the ladies because of its additional distance from the dining room. Adam sought to finish it all "in a style to afford great variety and amusement."[11] He divided the wall opposite the eleven windows into five bays centred on three pedimented doors and two chimneypieces, and the bold rhythm of his solution is reflected in the strong diagonals of the plasterwork ceiling. Bookshelves with pilasters of the Corinthian order, delicately painted by Pergolesi, and round-headed niches for sculpture on either side of the chimneypieces, create in effect the pattern of the triumphal arches. Flat-headed niches on either side of

A detail of the gilded pier table in the Red Drawing Room, typical of the refined delicacy of detail for which Adam was so admired in his lifetime

Part library, part withdrawing room, the Long Gallery was designed by Adam "in a style to afford variety and amusement." It was an adaptation of the sixteenth-century Long Gallery. There are sixty-two Corinthian pilasters decorated by Pergolesi.

The finely decorated Turret Room at the northeast end of the Long Gallery, which acted as a small boudoir or closet

the doors originally held vases. All the niches were later fitted as bookshelves, thus altering the intended effect of Adam's varied treatment of the long wall.

The Long Gallery was enlivened with delicate grotesque stuccowork and numerous paintings—those over the chimneypieces by Zuccarelli, and a series of thirty-six medallion portraits of the ancestors of the Percy family tracing them back to Charlemagne. The 1st Duke himself wrote of the fireplaces as "adorned with medallions after the most beautiful manner of the Antique finished in a remarkably light & elegant style at least equal, if not superior, to any of the finest remains of antiquity."[12] Mirror glass replaced the original overmantels. The little closets or cabinets, according to Adam, "served only for an additional amusement" and were decorated with fine plasterwork. They are known as the Turret Rooms today.

Beyond these great rooms also lay the private apartments, including the Duchess's bedchamber and a sequence of rooms for her maids, as well as an equivalent bedchamber and dressing rooms for the Duke. There were also plans for a huge circular saloon, which may originally have been for temporary erection for receptions in the courtyard. The private rooms of the family were remodelled in a sympathetically classical spirit in the nineteenth century and also accommodate a number of fine chimneypieces designed by Adam and furniture from the Percys' London house in the Strand, Northumberland House. Syon House remains undoubtedly one of the finest of Adam's realised interior schemes, an important chapter by any reckoning in the development of the English interior.

A needlework sofa of the 1760s, which came originally from the Tapestry Room at Northumberland House, the London house of the Percys that was sadly demolished in 1874

GOODWOOD HOUSE

The Regency Revolution in Taste

GOODWOOD HOUSE IN SUSSEX IS THE SEAT OF THE DUKES OF RICHMOND, who are descended from the son of Louise de Kéroualle and Charles II. The family acquired Goodwood near Chichester in the late seventeenth century as a hunting lodge, and it was gradually developed into the seat of a landed family. The house was hugely extended in 1800–06, and thus falls into the period known as Regency, after the regency of the Prince of Wales (later George IV) during the illness of his father, George III. The spur for the new works at Goodwood was partly the need of the 3rd Duke of Richmond to accommodate the vast collections of paintings and sculpture previously housed at Richmond

A detail of the late-eighteenth-century chimneypiece carved by John Bacon in the Tapestry Room at Goodwood House, Sussex

A view from across the park of Goodwood House, as extended by James Wyatt in the early 1800s, with round towers and the double-storey portico (Matthew Brettingham's 1740s wing can be seen to the left of the picture).

House, in Whitehall, London (Richmond House was destroyed by fire in 1791, although the art collection was mostly saved). In the Picturesque spirit of the age, the new house was also planned in a way that would make more of the breathtaking landscape setting.[1]

The 3rd Duke was a former army officer, politician, and onetime Whig who had championed the cause of the American colonists and the Irish but later become more conservative in his politics. In his youth he travelled in Italy on the Grand Tour, visiting ancient sites around Rome and also Herculaneum outside Naples. On his return he added a sculpture gallery to Richmond House designed by Sir William Chambers, who also designed the stables at Goodwood.

After seeing action at the Battle of Minden as an army officer in 1759, the 3rd Duke served as ambassador to Paris in 1765–66 (where, among other things, he commissioned a service from the Sèvres manufactory and was presented by Louis XV with a series of Gobelins tapestries depicting the *Life of Don Quixote*, around which the Tapestry Drawing Room at Goodwood was created in the late 1770s). Although a prominent politician in the 1780s and '90s, he fell out with the supporters of Pitt, lost his place in the government, and devoted his later years to making improvements to the house and estate at Goodwood in Sussex. He employed James Wyatt as his architect.

In fact, Wyatt had already remodelled part of the old house for him in the 1770s, and added the Tapestry Drawing Room, considered one of the finest neoclassical interiors, with a magnificent marble chimneypiece carved by John Bacon. Wyatt also designed the orangery and hunt kennels. Wyatt came

from a leading dynasty of builders and architects who developed one of the most influential architectural practices in England.[2] He had studied in Italy on his Grand Tour and rivalled Robert Adam as an early champion of the neo-classical style. His best-known classical works include Castle Coole in Ireland and the library at Oriel College, Oxford. He was also surveyor of Westminster Abbey and an admired practitioner of Regency Gothic, including the ill-fated Fonthill Abbey, the rebuilding of Belvoir Castle in Rutland, and Ashridge in Hertfordshire.

For the revived Goodwood, Wyatt moved towards the newly fashionable picturesque. He incorporated parts of the older house, including the Palladian hall designed by Roger Morris and an earlier 1740s wing by Matthew Brettingham, adding two new classical ranges with round corner towers, finished in grey, knapped flint. The middle range has the principal entrance at the centre, framed by a Portland stone portico with Doric columns on the ground floor and Ionic columns on the first floor.

The first Wyatt interior to be completed within the new house was the entrance hall, fitted with an elegant screen of columns of Guernsey granite, which the Duke's librarian, Dennett Jacques, described in 1822 as of the "most exquisite polish and form with rich bronzed Corinthian Capitals"[3] (at each end are two half columns in scagliola). The room was originally filled with bronze copies of antique Roman sculptures and is now hung with a fine collection

Wyatt's entrance hall at Goodwood, with a screen of Corinthian columns. The painting over the chimneypiece by Stubbs shows racehorses exercising at Goodwood.

of pictures, including paintings by Stubbs.[4] The second major interior to be finished before the 3rd Duke's death was the dining room, completed in 1806. The interiors of the whole sequence of rooms designed by Wyatt were completed for the 3rd Duke's great-nephew, the 5th Duke. The dining room was part of an ensemble that was among the richest in Regency England, which, partly because of the length of the decorating process, combined the eclecticism and deliberate contrasts in which designers and patrons delighted in that era with neo-Egyptian, neoclassical, and eighteenth-century French Rococo furniture styles. These styles were used to create rooms of quite different mood and brilliant grandeur, nonetheless always intended to be enjoyed en suite for great social events.

Contemporaries admired these interiors hugely. Diarist and M P Thomas Creevey visited in 1828 and wrote, "The House at Goodwood is perfection. It is an immense concern and every part of it is gaiety itself." Everything had been done, he said, in "perfect taste," and he admired especially the "principal drawing-room, 60 feet long at least I should say, with a circular room open at the end—both rooms furnished with the brightest yellow satin."[5] This drawing room has recently been carefully restored using evidence of the original work.

The Egyptian Dining Room was completed in 1806, and while much of the original decoration was lost, the overall decorative scheme was brilliantly restored in 1998 using available evidence. The result is unforgettable. Egyptian

overleaf The magnificently restored Egyptian Dining Room at Goodwood House, one of the most exotic interiors of Regency England when first completed in 1806. The walls are scagliola and the Egyptian details were drawn from Baron Denon's Planches du Voyage dans la Basse et la Haute Egypte pendant les Campagnes du général Bonaparte *(1802).*

revival style in decoration was a lively novelty, but was closely associated with classical architecture, not least through the presence of pyramids and obelisks in classical Rome. It was given a fresh impetus with the conquest of Egypt by Napoleon and, perhaps more excitingly for the English, Nelson's first great naval victory, the Battle of the Nile in 1798, which led to the defeat of Napoleon's army in Egypt the following year. Jacques referred to it in 1822, when talking about two vases in the library, which were "taken in a French frigate and once formed part of the plunder of the celebrated army of Egypt so nobly routed by the English and shamefully deserted by their head General Bounapart."[6]

The details in the Egyptian Dining Room have been traced to engravings in Vivant Denon's *Planches du Voyage dans la Basse et la Haute Eygpte pendant les Campagnes du général Bonaparte*, published in 1802, only two years before Wyatt's work on the dining room at Goodwood; other details seem to have

The Yellow Drawing Room revives the lost Regency scheme inspired by French taste. The curtain arrangement was reconstructed, and furniture was brought from elsewhere in the house (some items were copied) to accompany the 1830s gilded frames of the principal pier glasses in the room.

been taken from the engravings published by Piranesi. It is also likely that the room was influenced by the work of Thomas Hope, whose own house on Duchess Street with some neo-Egyptian interiors was already celebrated by this time, and which Wyatt had probably seen.

The real spectacle of the dining room was not just the architectural form and the detail, but the richness of the colour scheme: a warm yellow brown executed in a polished scagliola (a Mr. Joseph Allcot was paid £300 in 1804 for this work). A vivid description is given in Jacques's 1822 guidebook to Goodwood: "The walls are of scagliola, resembling a rich sienna marble, with a cornice and skirting of grey and white marble, adorned with Classical monuments in bronze."[7]

At the far end of the room, he wrote, there was "a large looking glass, nine feet by five, inserted in a fascia of grey marble, before which, on a pedestal, stands a vase of Egyptian porphyry; and on each side are side tables of choice granite" and "girandole figures of Isis and Osiris in bronze and gold." The backs of the chairs are mounted with bronze crocodiles. Jacques noted that the emperor of Russia was entertained here in this "superb room" in 1814. His guidebook also noted the presence of an Egyptian mummy in a glass case in the old dining room.

The Egyptian Dining Room had lost much of its original decoration and was restored with advice from Christopher Smallwood Architects and Lady Victoria Waymouth in 1998 for the Earl and Countess of March (the eldest son of the present Duke and his wife), who live at Goodwood today. Original furniture was returned, including the ormolu candelabra by Rundell, Bridge and Rundell in the Egyptian style. As former curator Rosemary Baird has written: "It is like a tomb cut in sandy-coloured rock. Illuminated at dusk or by night … it glitters and gleams."[8]

Wyatt's direct contribution ended in the early 1800s, but the work to the interiors continued to unfold, reflecting in different ways the 3rd Duke's original intentions and the changing tastes and styles of the Regency period. The 4th Duke, a soldier and governor-general of British North America (now Canada), died in 1819 and had little chance to make much contribution to the house at Goodwood, but his son, the 5th Duke, was eventually able to complete decorative work.

So he brought Wyatt's rooms to completion, including the Yellow Drawing Room, admired by Creevey, and also fully restored in 1998. This was always intended to house full-length portraits painted originally for Richmond House and framed in Kentian gilded frames, which hang there still. In 1839 William Hayley Mason wrote of the room: "The decoration and furniture are of the most elegant and costly description: the walls are hung in rich amber coloured silk tabouret, with full draperies to the three windows, and the luxuriant sofas, ottomans, couches and cabriole chairs are covered in the same material."[9]

A similar room survives at the Duke of Wellington's London home at Apsley House. The drawing room at Goodwood was restored using the evidence of inventories and mid-nineteenth-century photographs. Sadly, much of the original furniture, stored during the war, was destroyed in a fire, but it has been replaced with similar items from the collection.

The final major programme of work to the great Regency interiors was to the ballroom, still unfinished in 1836 but completed in 1838 by a Mr. Elliot

of Chichester. The 3rd Duke had always planned it as his picture gallery, even going to the length of sketching out the picture hang himself. The room was largely in the French revival style, evoking the rich rococo of Louis xv (although in England at the time this style was often mistakenly called the Louis-Quatorze Style), which was associated with late Regency and early Victorian interior design. The exuberance of this style is evident in the gilded frame to the huge mirror glass at one end of the ballroom, the carved and gilded pelmets, and the balustrade of the musician's gallery.

Goodwood House today, after a long programme of works carried out under the direction of the Earl and Countess of March, offers an unparalleled opportunity to enjoy the sequence of the famous Regency pursuit of comfort, good taste, and grandeur, ranging from the elegance of Louis xv's France to the rich, monumentalism of ancient Egypt.[10]

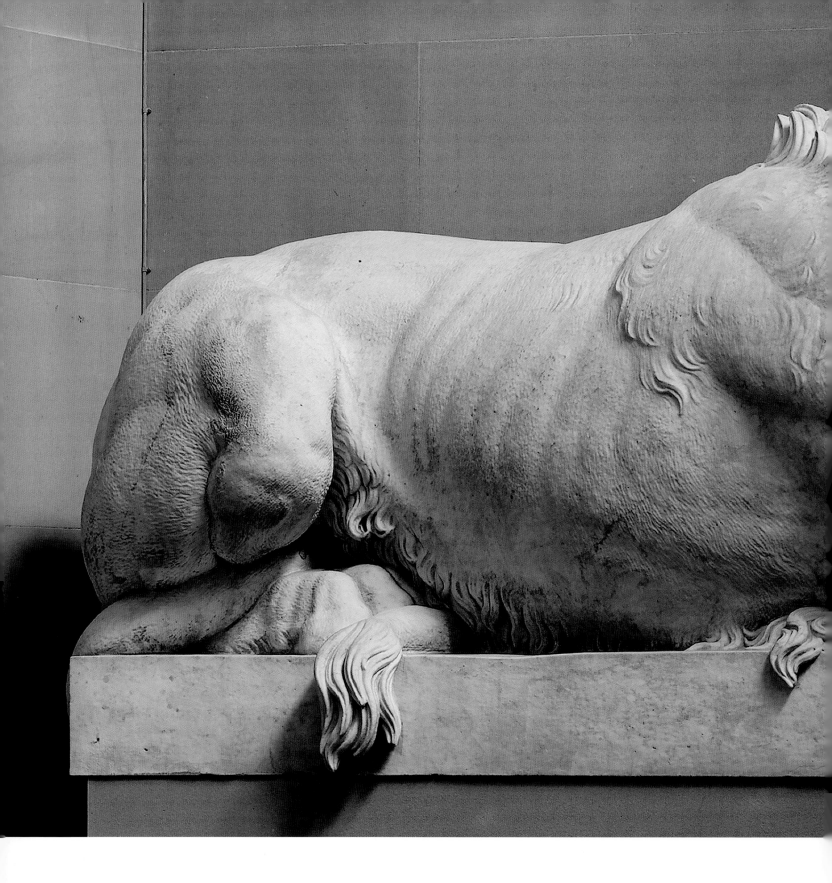

11 REGENCY REINVENTION

Some Houses Revisited

THE ENGLISH COUNTRY HOUSE WORLD WAS TRANSFORMED DURING the last years of the eighteenth century and early years of the nineteenth century. The formality and palace-like quality of the great country houses of the seventeenth and early eighteenth centuries gave way to something more like what we recognise today as a country house. The houses of the aristocracy were still grand and magnificent but were now arranged around the comfort of families and the country house parties that mixed informal country pursuits with formal dinners and balls, which became fashionable during this time.[1] The style of this period in England has been dubbed "Regency" after the period

A copy of one of Canova's lions in the magnificent sculpture gallery at Chatsworth, the high point of the Regency additions made by the 6th Duke of Devonshire

179

during the illness of George III, when his eldest son, the Prince of Wales (later George IV), himself a considerable patron of architecture and interiors, was regent. It should be treated as a loose term and is usually taken to reflect the 1790s to the 1830s, and has its parallel in the Federal style of the United States.

But, as we have seen at Goodwood House, which reflected the changing world and expanding horizons, the styles employed for architecture and interiors were increasingly wide-ranging. Indeed different styles were sometimes used to great effect in the same house, to create a different mood. At one end, there was an austere neoclassicism popular in some quarters, a progression from the work of Adam and Chambers, and influenced by ancient Roman, Greek, and Egyptian models, while the luxuriousness of French eighteenth century favoured by the Prince Regent (certainly before the French wars reached their height) also had a currency in the grandest houses. Meanwhile, Gothic was beginning to emerge as an attractive, and many felt more British, alternative to classical models, particularly during the years of isolation from the continent during the Napoleonic wars. Other styles of the era include Italianate, neo-Norman, Indian, and Chinese (as with the Royal Pavilion in Brighton).

This was a period of unprecedented prosperity and security for the landed aristocracy, and their houses remained centres for political and social life. Agricultural improvements and expanding trade consolidated aristocratic wealth—in these years before the Reform Acts began to reduce the power of the landed elite. Thus the country house party increased in popularity and demanded a larger number of reception rooms, with bedrooms for guests and family on the upper floors. At such parties, female guests would be encouraged to enjoy the opulent comfort of the interiors. Furniture was arranged throughout the room, with sofas, tables, and chairs placed for companionable activities, much as it still is today, rather than lined against the wall. This is the era of the library-come-living room. Prince Pückler-Muskau, a German aristocrat touring Britain in search of a rich wife, wrote of a stay at Cobham Hall in Kent that this style of entertainment was "the most agreeable side of English life for there is great freedom, and a banishment of most of the wearisome ceremonies, which, with us, tire both host and guest."[2]

Male guests would usually shoot or hunt, then join the ladies for a grand dinner party, which was by this time served in the evening rather than in the afternoon as had traditionally been the case. Luncheon was a new feature of life (and Pückler-Muskau refered to it as "a second breakfast"). For dinner parties, guests would assemble and process through the reception rooms to a large dining room, where liveried servants and displays of plate on sideboards added to the glamour. The *piano nobile* also ceased to be de rigeur, and the Regency landowner liked to be able to step out into the landscape. Many of the great houses already featured in this book as exemplars of the greatest interiors of particular periods were subject to radical remodellings with these changes in mind, and these shall provide our examples of Regency transformations.

The interiors of Wilton House were dramatically remodelled for the 11th Earl of Pembroke. The architect was James Wyatt, who also worked at Goodwood. He was engaged to modernise the house and to create more comfortable interiors reflecting just these changes to the country house way of life. Therefore at Wilton, Wyatt designed a new entrance hall to the north,

completed in 1809, and created a new two-tiered Gothic cloister to improve access between all the principal reception rooms, with plaster vaults by Francis Bernasconi, who also worked at Windsor Castle.[3]

The lower cloister was devoted to the passage of the servants, but the principal cloister level, described admiringly at the time as "stately and very light," was always intended as a striking sculpture gallery for the collections made by the 8th Earl of Pembroke (who acquired part of the Arundel collection in the 1680s and the Mazarin collection from Paris in the 1720s). In the upper lights, sixteenth-century stained glass was reset by Maria Eggington of Birmingham, who made additional sets of royal arms, and the colza oil lamps are part of early 1800s work. Wyatt also respected the admired interiors designed by Inigo Jones, only changing one of the main rooms on the south front to create an anteroom from the new cloister to the main state rooms, and introducing a new Gothic staircase between the *piano nobile* and the garden entrance.

Wyatt, by this time one of the busiest architects of the age, was notorious for losing control of his projects and was finally sacked in 1810. The final phase of Regency renewal at Wilton fell to the 11th Earl's second wife, Catherine Woronzow, daughter of Count Simon Woronzow (who had been Russian ambassador to Britain). With Mr. Fisher of Salisbury as clerk of works, and advice from the sculptor Richard Westmacott on the display in the cloisters, she completed the works at hand, and as John Martin Robinson has written: "It is thanks to her that Wilton combines the charm of an English country house with the splendour of a continental palace."[4]

Lady Pembroke also notably redecorated and furnished the state apartment

Wyatt created the Upper Cloisters, which were inserted into the quadrangle and were considered to have transformed the comfort and ease of circulation around Wilton House. The 8th Earl's sculpture collection was redisplayed around the cloisters, with advice from sculptor Richard Westmacott.

The entrance to the library at Arundel Castle, Sussex, built for the 11th Duke in 1801 to his own design inspired by the Perpendicular architecture of St. George's Chapel, Windsor. The carving was by Jonathan Ritson, Jr., and Jonathan Ritson, Sr.

in the 1820s in crimson, white, and gold, introducing the William Kent furniture (bought from the sale at Wanstead House) and having more pieces made to match. The huge sofa constructed under the great Van Dyck group portrait in the Double Cube Room is another of her confident touches. Her improvements showed how comfort and courtly elegance could be combined, expressing the contemporary taste for an opulent domesticity.

Arundel Castle, whose Victorian interiors will be discussed in chapter 12, had been subject to a major late-eighteenth-century programme of works by the 11th Duke of Norfolk, begun in the late 1790s and culminating in the early 1800s. This included the handsome Regency library and anteroom, which occupy part of the sixteenth-century Long Gallery (these two rooms survive intact today).5

The fashion for Gothic was well established in the late eighteenth century, often for national associations, as mentioned above, but also some, such as the 11th Duke, for its associations with historic freedoms. The 11th Duke included a Coade Stone relief showing *King Alfred Instituting Trial by Jury on Salisbury Plain* above the main entrance to the castle, and had stained glass made celebrating the Magna Carta for his new Great Hall, known as the Baron's Hall (the stone and stained glass were later replaced). Thus his interior work was executed in a style drawn mostly on Perpendicular Gothic—the Gothic of the late fifteenth and early sixteenth centuries. He also had an extensive programme of stained glass commissioned—the most extensive in any private house at that time.

Much of the 11th Duke's work, for which he was his own architect, was swept away in the late nineteenth century. However, the library, which in the spirit of many Regency interiors, was popular as a living room and retained. An article in *The Courier* described it thus in 1815: "The Library, which extends the whole length of the eastern side of the quadrangle, is of the present Duke's forming, his Grace's ancestors having left him few books. The receptacles for the books are also of his Grace's taste, and have been very lately finished. They are of the finest mahogany, modelled as it were, after the interiors of Westminster Abbey, with Gothic fret-work and other carving of the highest and most exquisite workmanship."6 The Duke's secretary, James Dallaway, asserted that it was in fact based on St. George's Chapel, Windsor.

The atmospheric interior is entirely fitted out in Honduras mahogany, and vaulted and aisled like the interior of a church, with galleries running along the whole length. The carving, of naturalistic leaves and berries, was all by Jonathan Ritson and his son, also Jonathan, who later went on to work at Petworth House in Sussex. The carved chimneypiece in the anteroom was added in the 1870s, designed carefully in the spirit of the early-nineteenth-century Gothic work, as with the carved doorcase. The fireplace alcoves at the centre of the Long Library, designed almost like chantry chapels, were added in the 1890s to designs by C. A. Buckler, who was the architect of the late-nineteenth-century rebuilding of much of the interiors of the castle, whose work is considered in chapter 12.

While Gothic was preferred in some quarters, during the Regency many new rooms were created in the neoclassical sprit, with simplified ornament and deliberately massive proportions. Castle Howard, for instance, received a major contribution to its interiors when the Long Gallery was created in 1801–11, even though the wing that it fills was added in the 1750s, designed

The Regency library at
Arundel was refurnished for
a visit of Queen Victoria in
1846, with a suite of red velvet
upholstered seat furniture
supplied by Morant & Co. The
curtains have been rehung as
they were shown in nineteenth-
century watercolours.

The Long Gallery at Castle Howard was designed by Charles Heathcote Tatham and retains its original pelmets and chimneypieces.

by Sir Thomas Robinson for the 4th Earl of Carlisle. The western wing was incomplete at the time of the 4th Earl's death, and was left unfinished until the 5th Earl was in a strong enough financial position to finish the gallery. He had already by then, however, made his name as a collector, and was (along with the Duke of Bridgwater, his father-in-law, and the 1st Marquess of Stafford, his brother-in-law) one of a triumvirate that had acquired a stake in the Italian and Dutch paintings of the Orleans collection.

Lord Carlisle had met the architect C. H. Tatham in Rome and commissioned him to finish the gallery in a dramatically austere, neoclassical taste.[7] It was executed in two phases: the southern section in 1801–02, and the northern section and central octagon a few years later. Reflecting contemporary neoclassical taste, the lofty gallery makes an interesting contrast with the intimate and highly finished rooms of the south front. The deliberate austerity of the space is lightened by the vaulting of the ceiling and the heavily curtained windows.

The central chimneypieces and side tables are in an Egyptian style, while the original pelmets with their Greek anthemion pattern also survive; busts on half-columns have always been a feature of the gallery. A delightful John Jackson painting of around 1812 shows the 5th Earl and one of his sons inspecting a painting on an easel in the gallery. On completion in 1811 Tatham published engravings of the gallery's internal elevations.[8]

A sculpture gallery of tremendous scale was also an important feature of the Regency additions made to Chatsworth. This was already one of the great show houses of England, but it was in many ways transformed by the 6th Duke of Devonshire, starting in 1818 and carrying on through to the 1830s. The 6th Duke, son of the famous Georgiana, was a high-minded and civilised individual who decided to renew the house. He restored and preserved the famous state rooms, while adding an impressive sequence of reception rooms on the north side of the house. The result is a perfect example of the Regency transformation of a Baroque palace to a country house built to entertain.⁹

The 6th Duke's architect was James Wyatt's nephew, Jeffry Wyatt (who later changed his name to Wyattville), who worked for George IV at Windsor Castle, the Dukes of Beaufort at Badminton in Gloucestershire, and the Marquess of Bath at Longleat, Wilthsire. The 6th Duke, who wrote his privately published account of the history of the house that included a description of his own alterations, noted that: "Sir Jeffry managed the additions to the house most admirably. My wish expressed to him was to have a suite of rooms, especially a good dining-room, in this direction [on the north side of the house]."

The old Long Gallery was completely transformed into a new library, which became one of the principal drawing rooms of the house (and is still used today). The ceiling was retained, and mahogany bookcases were created on three sides of the room, with a gallery running around the room ("very useful

The Long Gallery was completed within the existing unfinished wing in 1811; the bookcases were added in the 1820s.

Originally the 1st Duke of
Devonshire's Long Gallery,
the library at Chatsworth was
transformed for the 6th Duke
after 1818.

Completed in 1832, the magnificent dining room was designed by Jeffry Wyattville as part of a suite of rooms for entertaining house parties.

and convenient") and a huge statuary marble chimneypiece as the centrepiece.

The library was used as a room to gather when there were more than twenty-two guests for dinner. If there were twenty-two or fewer, guests gathered in the room known as the ante-library, a tribune decorated with classical columns: two of *giallastro* and two of *pavonazzetto*. The 6th Duke was enthusiastic about full plate-glass windows, observing: "The clear glasses were the first I placed here: they are the greatest ornament of modern decoration. Nothing struck me so much in Russia as the vast windows of single panes."[10] From the Ante-Library guests would progress through the dome room, where the 1827 wing joins the old house, and then to the Great Dining Room itself.

The Great Dining Room, the 6th Duke felt, "Answers perfectly, never feeling over large." Although he conceded that the proportions and the barrel-vaulted coffered ceiling gave the feeling of "dining in a trunk, and you expect the lid to open. In this age of ornament and decoration the lines appear too straight."[11] The doors are framed between coloured marble columns, acquired from Richmond House, while the chimneypieces were carved by Westmacott and Sievier with lifesize Bacchic figures, which the 6th Duke later wrote were not expressive enough.

The high point of the Regency additions to Chatsworth is the magnificent top-lit sculpture gallery, which was created especially for the 6th Duke, who was an influential collector of modern sculpture, particularly the work of Antonio Canova, the most famous neoclassical sculptor and a close friend of the 6th Duke's.[12] The Duke had busts of himself and Canova placed in the niches at the western end, above copies of the lions made by Canova for the tomb of Pope Clement XIII at St. Peter's in Rome. He also owned Canova's bust of Napoleon and the sculpture of Napoleon's sister, Pauline Borghese. Other artists represented included Thorvaldsen, Tenerani, and the Prussian Schadow. In 2008–09 the sculpture was returned to the original arrangement laid down by the 6th Duke and can be enjoyed as it was first conceived.

The 6th Duke wrote himself that: "My Gallery was intended for modern sculpture, and I have almost entirely abstained from mixing it with any fragments of antiquity: it was in vain to hope for time or opportunities of collecting really fine ancient marbles. In addition to the statues, my wish was to obtain rare coloured marbles as pedestals for them."[13] He acquired different columns of modern and ancient marble, and pedestals for busts, and had them all repolished at Ashford marble mills. The sculpture gallery has been returned to its original arrangement by the 6th Duke.[14]

In 2011 the 6th Duke's guest bedrooms were also returned to their 1830s furnishings.[15] Greater attention has been given throughout to the remarkable survival of the Regency country house interior, with its combination of elegance and comfort. For many who visit country houses today, it is interiors of this period, with their emphasis on glamour and entertainment, that appeal most fully to the modern imagination.

overleaf The 6th Duke's sculpture gallery is filled with his collection of neoclassical pieces by contemporary sculptors, especially Canova. The sculptures were recently re-presented in the same positions they were in the 1850s.

12 ARUNDEL CASTLE

The Gothic Revival Interior

THERE ARE FEW GREAT COUNTRY HOUSES THAT SO PERFECTLY exemplify the nineteenth-century Romantic taste for the medieval forms of architecture and interior decoration as Arundel Castle in Sussex. Founded in 1067, Arundel Castle is an ancient place in its own right, and the curtain wall and gatehouse that survive today date from about 1070, while the keep is from 1140. It was subject to a series of alterations, but none so dramatic and all-encompassing as those done for Henry Fitzalan-Howard, the 15th Duke of Norfolk (1847–1917), who came of age in 1868. With the employment of architect Charles Buckler, a follower of the Gothic Revival values of A.W.N. Pugin,

A detail of the vaulted ceiling of chalk and Painswick stone over the Grand Staircase at Arundel Castle, Sussex, designed by C. A. Buckler for the 15th Duke of Norfolk

this work was an artistic triumph, as witnessed by anyone who has seen the spectacular, picturesque outline of the castle across the landscape. The building was described by historian Mark Girouard as "enormous, feudal, ducal."[1]

The later-nineteenth-century Gothic Revival interiors of Arundel could certainly be described as just that. The style employed had an additional intensity and zestfulness derived from the 15th Duke's role as the premier Catholic peer and hereditary Earl Marshall (in which role he served Queen Victoria). The Duke was a considerable architectural enthusiast with deeply scholarly tastes, although he was barred from attending Cambridge as a Roman Catholic. He had already commissioned and built a vast Gothic Revival Catholic church, Our Lady and St. Philip Neri, completed in 1873 to designs by Joseph Hansom (now designated a full cathedral). In fact, the 15th Duke was patron of numerous building projects including Roman Catholic churches in England and Canada. He also co-founded St. Edmund's House (now Hall) in Cambridge.[2]

Such was the potency of Romantic historicism in the nineteenth century that there had already been attempts to remodel the castle in the medieval spirit, as we have seen in chapter 11. The Romantic Movement, from the novels of Sir Walter Scott to the paintings of Turner, all contributed to a sense of pride in England's Gothic inheritance. This was also intensified by the isolation of the Napoleonic blockade that interrupted the long tradition of the Grand Tour, which had underlined so much of the architecture and decoration of the previous two centuries. The decorative Gothic of the Regency era was, however, considered superficial by figures such as A.W.N. Pugin, and the subsequent generations of architects and designers approached the Gothic with a greater seriousness, as we can see at Arundel.

The 15th Duke wanted to continue the revival of the castle that had been initiated by his beloved father, who had died young in 1860. He wanted to do this work so well that it would last for a thousand years. He searched hard for the right architect and deliberately chose Charles Buckler, a herald and scholarly architect with an immense knowledge of English medieval architecture.

Arundel Castle's Romantic outline as seen across the Sussex countryside. It is composed of both ancient and Victorian elements and yet seems a very complete work of art.

Buckler was also a co-religionist, a Roman Catholic convert from a dynasty of antiquarian artists. Together they devised a spirited restoration that was as thorough in the thirteenth-century Gothic spirit of its interiors as in its architecture. It was a project spread out over twenty years, costing £570, 377.17s.10d—the equivalent of some £50 million today.[3]

In order to make additions to the castle that would both honour its history and add to its Romantic presence in the landscape, Buckler made a special study of the ancient castles of the country, especially Bodiam Castle and Pevensey Castle in Sussex. While Buckler was undoubtedly the architect of the new works to the castle, the 15th Duke himself was closely involved, and there is evidence to show that he personally approved almost every detail, material, and colour employed at Arundel Castle.

A constant stream of sketch designs were sent to the 15th Duke for his approval, and various treatments for towers and chimneys were first tried out in timber cutouts for his inspection. Together they took immense pleasure in sourcing workable decorative details from historic medieval examples, not least in the heraldic entitlements of the family, down to such details as the Fitzalan acorns and oak leaves on the hinges of oak doors. The 15th Duke himself came up with practical ideas too, such as the use of gunmetal for the casement windows, which was more robust and did not corrode.

The 15th Duke certainly revelled in good craftsmanship and wanted to modernise the castle's services and make it as comfortable as he could with the technology of the day. The house was as up to date as any country house in terms of plumbing (with steam-pumped water supply, hydraulic lift,

The coat of arms of the 15th Duke, impaled with those of his first wife, Lady Flora Abney-Hastings, is carved on the chimneypiece in the drawing room (left) and the Norfolk arms since the sixteenth century on the Grand Staircase (right).

The stylish chimneypiece in the anteroom to the Long Library, designed by Buckler in the 1870s in sympathy with the Regency Gothic of the Long Library, is loaded with heraldic decoration.

The drawing room was created in the 1870s and remains a most magnificent room, redecorated in recent years to accommodate gilded furniture originally from Norfolk House.

and electricity). The 15th Duke also made considerable use of many of the great firms associated with A.W.N. Pugin's mid-nineteenth-century work in reviving serious Gothic detail, such as Hardman's of Birmingham and Dunstan Powell (Pugin's son-in-law) for metalwork and stained glass; Thomas Earp of Cheltenham for stone carving; Rattee and Kett of Cambridge for joinery; Minton of Stoke-on-Trent for encaustic tiles; and Crace for fabrics. As Arundel's historian and the current Duke's librarian, John Martin Robinson, has written: "Arundel is Pugin's ideal made solidly manifest."[4]

Pugin was a standard-bearer for Gothic Revival from the 1840s and '50s, and his designs for the Palace of Westminster set the standard for imaginative re-creations in the Gothic spirit; he was also a Roman Catholic convert who had argued for the Gothic as the true Christian style. In his passionate and persuasive publications he denounced the foreignness and secular character of classical architecture and added a sense of fire to the already strong antiquarian tradition in England, as represented by Buckler's father, and indeed by himself and his brother. Buckler's Gothic is noticeably scholarly and English in character. The work at Arundel Castle was divided into two phases: first in the 1870s, then again in the 1890s. It was disrupted by the tragic death in 1887 of the 15th Duke's young wife, Lady Flora Abney-Hastings, and the serious illness of their only son, Philip, who was handicapped from birth and died young in 1902. The 15th Duke was married again in 1907, to Gwendoline Maxwell-Constable, with whom he had four more children.

Of the works completed in the 1870s, the most important was probably the drawing room, which is dominated by the hooded chimneypiece carved by Thomas Earp. The oak ceiling and its carved cornice with numerous painted coats of arms were supplied in 1879 by Rattee and Kett. Buckler himself researched the coats of arms, which show all the quarterings brought to the Howard family by marriages to heiresses from the late thirteenth to the nineteenth centuries.

It was intended originally to paint the stone walls of this room in the manner of Henry III's Great Hall at Winchester with a pattern of red lines and scrolls, but this was not carried out (although the picture rails were painted white and red). In the windows are cast-iron curtain "cranes" that allowed curtains to be used within the Gothic windows, which, being arched, could not easily carry a pelmet, an ingenious device based on medieval precedents.

The Grand Staircase is also in the early English style and is rich in architectural detail and atmospheric light cast by the tall lancet windows. The latter are filled with stained glass with borders in the colours of the Norfolk livery of red, white, and gold. The staircase—with its pierced stone quatrefoils, polished Derbyshire marble handrail, and heraldic lions carved by Thomas Earp—is contained within a soaring space, which takes the eye upwards to the dramatic vaulted ceiling. The carved stone decoration combines Catholic Christian imagery and heraldic decoration.

The work completed in the 1890s included the dining room, created on the site of the medieval chapel, as well as a new chapel and the vast Baron's Hall—a deliberate evocation of the medieval Great Hall. The 15th Duke also collected suitable oak furniture and carved oak and walnut cabinets and tables, as well as early paintings—including a rare Flemish triptych from the Beresford-Hope collection—and arms and armour.[5]

As surviving sixteenth-century English furniture of the best quality was so rare, the 15th Duke eagerly collected continental furniture of the type described in the original sixteenth-century inventory of the castle, much of it bought for him by Charles Davis, a Bond Street dealer. He spent £6,717 with Davis in 1883 alone. The paintings in the Baron's Hall mix medieval altar paintings, early portraits, and history paintings, including Mather Brown's painting of *The Earl of Surrey Defending His Allegiance before Henry VII*.

The chapel and the Baron's Hall were both visual celebrations of the family's own long history as English landowners faithful to the Roman Catholic Church. The Baron's Hall was a deliberate resurrection of the medieval Great

One of the most original interiors of Victorian Arundel, the dining room replaced the eighteenth-century chapel.

Hall of the Fitzalans, Earls of Arundel, on a scale that could dwarf a substantial country house—perhaps scaled deliberately to outshine those great halls and saloons of the Palladian and neoclassical houses. It was modelled on the Great Hall at Penshurst and the Guesten Hall at Worcester Cathedral, with the ceiling influenced by that of Westminster Hall. The hooded chimneypieces were sourced in the publications of French nineteenth-century architect Viollet-le-Duc, and the windows decorated with heraldic glass.[7] The furnishings in the Baron's Hall were almost all acquired by the 15th Duke in the 1880s and largely are still in the positions in which he placed them.

The ecclesiastical character of the dining room is unmistakable. The 15th Duke had first thought of rebuilding the chapel here, so the lancet windows originated from that idea. The room was given a strongly architectural character, with tall windows and a vaulted ceiling from which electric chandeliers hang on black chains in suitably Gothic mood. The heraldic tiles in the fireplace are Minton. Buckler also redesigned the long picture gallery, first created in the early eighteenth century and later refaced with Painswick stone and given a vaulted ceiling, with Gothic tracery and stained glass in the windows.

The new chapel was first conceived in the 1870s but was not actually begun until 1894. Completed in 1898, it is a major masterpiece of Victorian Gothic and has been called the 15th Duke's "Sainte Chappelle."[8] Typical of the scholarly approach of the Duke and his architect, the chapel is based on the design of the lost chapel of Henry III, which used to stand at the east end of Westminster Abbey and was replaced by Henry VII's famous chapel. The chapel is rich with Purbeck and Frosterly marbles.

above left A brilliant Gothic Revival design, the chapel was completed in 1894, every detail carefully based on thirteenth-century examples.

above right The Baron's Hall, a vast Great Hall designed by Buckler, was built in 1893–98 and furnished with English and Continental oak furniture.

The stained-glass art by Hardman was directly inspired by the early English glass at Canterbury Cathedral depicting the life of the Virgin Mary, which is echoed in the carvings of the stone bosses. The 15th Duke's own monument is, however, found in the nave of the historic Fitzalan Chapel, where he lies in medieval state with a bronze effigy by Sir Bertram Mackennal, showing him almost in the manner of an ecclesiastic.

In 1902 Sir Almeric Fitzroy recorded his impressions of the completed works at Arundel Castle: "We spent Sunday at Arundel, a place where the traditions of a stately and reverent life still survive. The castle has been restored by the present owner with a scrupulosity of sentiment it is impossible to praise too highly. The assimilation of the spirit of the past has taken the place of the sterile reproduction of its letter ... [both] elevating and subduing the mind to the reception of the most living lessons of history."[9]

The interiors of Arundel Castle are some of the finest examples of Gothic Revival work in the country that also survive with much of their original collections and the vision of their creation still largely intact. Many of the grand eighteenth-century furnishings and picture collections came from Norfolk House in London, but some of the great rooms at Arundel Castle remain hardly changed from the 15th Duke's time. Much of the recent work for the present Duke, advised by John Martin Robinson, David Mlinaric, and others, has helped reveal the consistency and quality of the late-nineteenth-century work.[10] It has made these grand Gothic rooms especially comfortable and elegant, including a series of private rooms: billiard room, dining room, and drawing room, which will be considered in chapter 16 of this book.

13 WADDESDON MANOR

The Inspiration of the Chateau

WADDESDON MANOR IN BUCKINGHAMSHIRE IS ONE OF THE GREATEST
Victorian mansions in England to survive with its original interiors intact.
It is an astonishing house, and on the long, meandering approach, it seems
to rise slowly like a chateau from a dream. Its interiors still have an air of
almost unnerving perfection. One late-nineteenth-century visitor wrote:
"Waddesdon is a marvellous creation; a real creation—not an old mansion
taken over with its gardens, park and stabling—but a vast chateau built by its
present owner, surrounded by endless gardens planted by him."[1] The creator
was a thoroughly cosmopolitan figure, the Baron Ferdinand Rothschild
(1839–1898).

*A detail of the curtain and
tassel in the state bedroom
at Waddesdon Manor,
Buckinghamshire*

Born in Paris then raised in Frankfurt and Vienna, Rothschild eventually settled in England. From a family of financiers with an international reputation as art collectors, Rothschild himself was assiduous in the pursuit of the art and objets for his new house at Waddesdon. He bought English, Dutch, and Italian paintings; French furniture, porcelain, and sculpture; and Renaissance treasures in gold, although surprisingly perhaps, little in the way of French eighteenth-century paintings or modern paintings. He was also buying while so many of the British aristocracy were selling off treasures. He was able therefore to acquire pieces from the Dukes of Hamilton, Buccleuch, Devonshire, and Rutland, and the Earls Spencer. He bought from many great continental collections as well, including from the Villa Demidoff near Florence.

Collecting is a key part of the story of the interiors at Waddesdon Manor, for it was always intended as a treasure house for the display of art and the reception of distinguished guests who would enjoy being shown these works of art. These guests would have appreciated the part that the art and period furniture he collected played in the elegance and refinement of the interiors of the house. In the tradition of English country house collections, things were to be used as part of a domestic ensemble and not confined to galleries.

Rothschild hugely admired the richness of the taste of George IV, writing that "the acclimatisation of French art might have been only temporary had not the Prince Regent … settled its destiny in this country. He was endowed with the most exquisite taste." Rothschild also felt that "He made Windsor Castle and Buckingham Palace storehouses of art treasures, and trained a school of collectors who profited by his example."[2] The latter included the 3rd Marquess of Hertford, whose collection was continued by his son, the 4th Marquess, and forms the core of the famous Wallace Collection today. (Rothschild was a friend of Sir Richard Wallace, who had inherited the collection.)

The foundation stone for Waddesdon Manor was laid in 1877 and it was

Waddesdon Manor from the garden. This French Renaissance chateau, designed especially for Baron Ferdinand Rothschild, was built in two stages in the 1870s and 1890s.

largely complete in the early 1880s. Designed by a French architect, Gabriel-Hippolyte Destailleur, in the manner of a magnificent sixteenth-century French chateau, Waddesdon Manor was inspired especially by the chateaux of the Valois kings, even though Rothschild chose to decorate the interiors in a more eighteenth-century spirit suited to his interests and the comfort associated with his hospitality. The son of an architect who had trained with Charles Percier, Destailleur was trained at the Ecole des Beaux-Arts. Like his father, Destailleur worked for the duc d'Orléans and was an authority on historic French architecture.

When Rothschild came to England, he had married a cousin, Evelina, the daughter of Lionel Rothschild. Her father was also a pioneer collector of English portraits and furnished his home with period French furniture. Evelina sadly died young, so Ferdinand Rothschild entertained without the support of a wife, but still filled the house with parties of famed luxury between May and September. There were many visits from the then Prince of Wales (later Edward VII), as well as political figures such as Gladstone, Balfour, and many others. Such entertainments were lavishly catered, and guests were taken on tours of the treasures of the house, the gardens, and the park.

Michael Hall in *Waddesdon Manor* (2002) has noted that while Waddesdon Manor has often been described as a manifestation of a Rothschild style, Baron Ferdinand was thought at the time to stand out among his Rothschild cousins for his superior aesthetic taste.[3] He was a member of the Souls group, a loose association during the 1890s of aristocrats, politicians, and art lovers, which included the Wyndhams, the Grenfells, Lord Curzon, and Violet, the Duchess of Rutland, and laid a heavy emphasis on good taste and discernment. Eustace Balfour wrote of Waddesdon: "The panelling and the tapestries, the hangings and the marbles were all one more beautiful than the other, and the whole in exquisite taste."[4] While Destailleur must have contributed ideas for interior design, there seems not to be another interior decorator involved, though Rothschild's controlling eye can be seen everywhere. The house was celebrated in *Country Life* in 1902, where it was observed: "there is no fear of brilliant colour; it is an eminently cheerful and inspiriting interior."[5]

Rothschild's interest in art could be traced back to his childhood. He recalled helping pack up some pieces from his father's collection so they could be moved to their villa at Grüneburg for the summer: "as soon as the swallows made their appearance.... It was my privilege on these occasions to place some of the smaller articles in their old leather cases, and then again in the winter to assist in unpacking of them and rearranging them in their places. Merely to touch them sent a thrill of delight through my small frame."[6] His mother taught him at a young age to distinguish the work of different painters.

The decoration of the house is especially interesting for the way that Rothschild created interiors of an appropriate richness for the first-rate treasures he wished to display; indeed some of the decoration was collected itself, for he acquired numerous eighteenth-century French boiseries, or carved decorative panelling, mostly from Parisian *hôtels particuliers* (private town houses). His desire was to create interiors of appropriate authenticity of detail and character for the art and furniture they contained.

The ground floor rooms of Waddesdon Manor are balanced between the private collector's paradise and rooms of reception suitable for his guests. Destailleur provided drawings for the incorporation of the old boiseries, and

The Small Library, where Baron Ferdinand Rothschild kept his books on history and the arts

different firms were used for the supply of the rich textiles, such as Decour in Paris and specialist carpet dealers such as Pluyette. Antique textiles helped contribute to a mellowness of effect, and Rothschild was not averse to using eighteenth-century dress silks to cover chairs with new passementerie.[7]

The east and west galleries were panelled in dark oak boiseries, against which paintings, textiles, and marble sculpture are displayed. The central room of the house, lying between the hall and the garden, is the Red Drawing Room, the first room of reception that his visitors would have seen. This jewel-like room is something of an homage to those who inspired his collecting, with a full-length portrait of George IV by Gainsborough and a marble relief of Louis XIV by Antoine Coysevox over the door to the hall. The richly coloured Savonnerie carpet was woven in 1683 for Louis XIV for the Long Gallery at the Louvre. Also in the Red Drawing Room hang some of Rothschild's best English paintings, including Gainsborough's portrait of Lady Sheffield, as well as the best Sèvres porcelain and Jean-Henri Riesener commodes made for the French royal family.

The Grey Drawing Room next door is panelled with eighteenth-century boiserie from the hotel Peyrenc de Moras, which is now the Musée Rodin in Paris. One of the two rooms that can be regarded almost as reconstructions, it is painted a light grey-blue (the panelling was originally painted in a *couleur*

A view through the Red Drawing Room into the marble-lined dining room: the delicious contrast of the crimson damask and the varied colours of the marble is highly effective.

d'eau). It is furnished with another set of superb French furniture, including pieces inset with Sèvres panels and a chest of drawers mounted in gilt bronze with branches, birds, and putti climbing in the branches, acquired from the Hamilton Palace sale in 1882. The walls are hung with a series of portraits of famous beauties by Sir Joshua Reynolds.[8] In planning such rooms, Destailleur also often had casts taken of the original plasterwork to create an appropriate ceiling decoration at Waddesdon Manor.

The dining room is a wonderfully elegant room capable of seating some forty-two diners. Inspired by Louis XIV's state apartments at Versailles, the walls are lined in mauvy-grey variegated marble, on which hang two large tapestries woven at Beauvais to designs by François Boucher from a series of five called *La Noble Pastorale*. A series of delicately carved gilded mirror frames came from the Hôtel des Villars in Paris, designed by Nicolas Pineau, one of the influential designers of the rococo style. Rothschild employed a famous chef, Auguste Chalanger, and a confectioner, Arthur Chategner, who had worked for the Russian tsar, and food was served using eighteenth-century porcelain.

The more private rooms include the Small Library, where Rothschild kept contemporary books and porcelain sculptures from Dresden. The breakfast room and first-floor Green Boudoir are panelled in a set of stripped and gilded

The Grey Drawing Room was fitted with eighteenth-century panelling bought from the salon of a town house (now the Musée Rodin) in the St. Germain district of Paris. The paintings are all portraits of famous women by Reynolds.

above *The White Drawing Room, part of the 1990–95 restoration programme instigated by Lord Rothschild, using French eighteenth-century boiseries probably first bought for Ferdinand Rothschild's London home but kept in store. The silver service on display was originally commissioned by George III.*

boiseries from the town house of Pierre Dodun, designed by Jean-Baptiste Bullet de Chamblin.

At the core of the original 1870s house lies the Baron's Room, Rothschild's private domain, which has recently been refurnished exactly as it was in Rothschild's life, with densely grouped furniture, including Moorish coffee tables and French eighteenth-century pieces and porcelain. The magnificent marquetry roll-top desk was made for Pierre-Auguste Caron de Beaumarchais, the author of *The Marriage of Figaro*, and there is also a drop-front *secrétaire* made by Riesener for Louis XVI's study at the Petit Trianon in 1777.

From this room is approached the yet more private Tower Drawing Room, Rothschild's original "*salle des curisosités*," where he had the real treasures of his collection, largely of medieval or Renaissance date. In the early 1880s, the Tower Room was described in a letter by Eustace Balfour as "hung entirely with magnificent Italian needlework, and quite full of old Venetian glass set in silver gilt, and other beautiful pieces of metal and gold plate."[9] When he later transferred the collection to the smoking room, Rothschild repanelled the Tower Drawing Room in neoclassical panelling of the 1770s, designed by Etienne-Louis Boullé.

In 1889–91 Rothschild extended Waddesdon Manor with the same architect, creating the Morning Room, essentially to allow his house party guests

right *The magnificent dining room, with five mirror frames designed in the 1730s by Nicolaus Pineau for the Paris house of the Duc de Villars*

overleaf, left, clockwise from top left *Textures and treasures: terra-cotta figures against the gold-coloured silk in the Morning Room; Sèvres porcelain on display; a centrepiece in the dining room; the marble wine cooler in the anteroom to the dining room*

overleaf right *Details of fine antique textile curtains in which the interiors of Waddesdon Manor are so rich, from the Red Drawing Room, Grey Drawing Room, and dining room*

additional space, or as he said, "a place were my friends could all meet, and read and write without disturbing each other."[10] The room is hung with a golden silk damask, with the especially carved bookcases gilded and the magnificent plasterwork ceiling completed in eighteenth-century style. The pictures in the room are Dutch Old Masters. The chairs are mostly covered with Beauvais tapestry. The Savonnerie carpets were made for Louis XV, while the huge *secrétaire* was acquired from the Hon. George Fitzwilliam's collection.

Bachelor guests' accommodation was provided in a dedicated bachelor wing, with a smoking room and billiard room for their especial use (remodelled in 1896). The interiors of both these rooms are in a more Renaissance style, matching the exterior architecture. The smoking room, again recently restored, housed a sampling of Rothschild's *cinquecento* treasures; Limoges enamels and majolica; and precious metals and minerals (many of which he left to the British Museum).[11]

The billiard room is an especially handsome and masculine space, lined with Renaissance boiseries from the chateau of Acquigny, built in the 1560s. The room is vaulted in the late-fifteenth-century style with stamped and gilded leather between the ribs. The overmantel is an elegantly carved, sixteenth-century frieze showing terms holding children and swags of fruit.

The interiors at Waddesdon Manor are dazzling but also more subtle than

is often acknowledged. Rothschild left the house and estate to his sister, Alice, who later left it to her great-nephew, James de Rothschild, and his wife, Dorothy. Both Alice and Dorothy initiated regimes of housekeeping designed to preserve the textiles and colours of the marquetry. Dorothy and the National Trust also thinned out furniture before opening it to the public, to show the better pieces more clearly, removing comfortable nineteenth-century seat furniture.[12]

In 1957 the house was left to the National Trust, and it is now managed by the Alice Trust. During the 1990s this special family trust, chaired by the present Lord Rothschild, initiated a number of important restorations and new rooms and displays in the continuing spirit of Ferdinand Rothschild's inspired nineteenth-century chateau of art. Waddesdon Manor is a demonstration of what could be achieved with wealth and a connoisseur's knowledge, reflecting the nineteenth-century pleasure in the art of the past, adapted to the needs of the present.

The billiard room, restored in the 1990s. The panelling and detailing reflected the more consciously Renaissance character of the Bachelor's Wing.

14 BERKELEY CASTLE

The Castle of Taste

THE PAST PROVIDES A COMPELLING PALETTE FOR THE ENGLISH
interior, and modernism played more of a role in urban design in the early
twentieth century than in the country house. The characteristic country house
interior of the early twentieth century was founded not in a desire for novelty
but in a combination of antiquarian and Aesthetic Movement values. The
most interesting decoration was as likely to be found as part of a restoration
of an old country house or castle. The glamour of the ancient medieval castle
held a special place in the minds of the early-twentieth-century aristocrat, and
many older houses received attention for the first time in centuries.[1]

*Carved figures on the door
to the Great Hall, Berkeley
Castle. The 8th Earl Berkeley
acquired the doors in France
and installed them during his
major restoration of the house
in the 1920s.*

221

This admiration derived partly from the values of the Gothic revival, which honoured the medieval tradition, as we have seen at Arundel Castle. The values of Ruskin and Morris that contributed to the Arts and Crafts Movement, which celebrated the importance of the genuinely authentic medieval survival. Modern writers tend to emphasise the rejection of new design in old styles developed by Morris and his followers, but the huge impact that their thinking and approach had on Aesthetic Movement artists, and the increased celebration of old and beautiful buildings—even celebrating the old and worn tapestry and furniture of ancient houses—cannot be underestimated.[2]

Berkeley Castle in Gloucestershire is of Norman origin but was largely rebuilt in the fourteenth century following the existing outline and continued to be altered in later centuries. This gave it an organic, sculptural quality, almost like a ruin in a watercolour painting. Gertrude Jekyll at the beginning of the century caught this quality when she wrote that it seemed "like some great fortress roughly hewn out of natural rock … when the day is coming to its close, and the light becomes a little dim and thin mist-films arise from the meadows, it might be an enchanted castle, for in some tricks of evening light it cheats the eye into something ethereal, without substance, built up for the moment into towering masses of pearly vapour."[3] This sense of the admiration for the Picturesque also had its application to the interiors of such houses, with their evocative great halls and panelled rooms.

Berkeley Castle has been owned by the same family for over eight centuries (a family of considerable influence, including the founder of the University of California, Berkeley). In 1916 it was inherited by Randal Berkeley, the

Berkeley Castle, Gloucestershire, as seen from its terraced gardens. The castle has Norman origins but was mostly built in the fourteenth century.

8th Earl of Berkeley (1865–1942), a former naval officer and scientist, and a Fellow of the Royal Society, who studied osmosis in his own private laboratory near Oxford. His house on Boars Hill was redesigned for him in 1904–06 by Sir Ernest George. Weighing the needs of the remaining estate and castle at Berkeley, Lord Berkeley resolved to sell family properties in London and devote some of the moneys raised, in his own words "to transform the castle into the most beautiful in England."[4]

The revival and redecoration of the castle was already well on its way in 1924 when he married his second wife, Mary Lowell, a Bostonian who had trained as an artist and lived in Italy. She may well have influenced the final comfortable and artistic finish of many of the rooms. In Italy she had worked on frescoes in old chapels and persuaded the 8th Earl to buy a villa just outside Rome, which by the early 1930s had become their principal project. They also had a house in Santa Barbara, California, where, to complete the thoroughly Wodehousian life they led, they played golf.[5]

There is a Henry Jamesian air to the 8th Earl's interiors (which have echoes of the description of the fictional house in *The Spoils of Poynton*). There is also a touch of the Italian *palazzo* style at Berkeley, suggested by such things as the presence of Venetian lamps in the Great Hall and the furnishing of the morning room.

The 8th Earl's obituarist in the *Journal of the Royal Society* (1942), remarked: "He [Lord Berkeley] once went to Crete with Arthur Evans to help in the excavations at Knossos, and the work at Berkeley was planned with the same scrupulous accuracy in the attempt to discover the exact lines of the earlier buildings, and to unearth every fragment of the original masonry and timber and restore it to its original position…. Berkeley was his own architect, every detail of the work had to be approved by him."[6]

Intent on discovering every bit of old carved masonry and woodwork, the 8th Earl "used to carry a small hand-pick to test any plaster he could find [revealing for instance the huge timbers of the Small Drawing Room] … [but] It soon became evident that in spite of the most careful search there were many gaps to be filled and Berkeley, who was by then immensely interested in Gothic tracery, began to hunt in England, France and Italy for suitable windows, doors and panelling to fill the empty spaces. Stone doorways came from Lorraine, linenfold panelling from East Anglia, doors from Paris and Florence, and chimneypieces from old houses on the estate."

His obituarist acknowledged that purists might have objected to the insertion of things from elsewhere, but "only after every vestige of the best had been salved did Berkeley give rein to his fancy." Lady Berkeley, however, recalled her husband having an absolute mania for building projects: "If you went away for a few days, you'd come back to find the side of your room had been taken off and all the furniture moved out."[7] His stated intention was to reveal the ancient beauty of the castle, but he, admittedly, did this through a number of alterations, in some cases stripping away Georgian and Victorian alterations, including panelling.[7]

The 8th Earl seems to have taken an inordinate amount of trouble himself in directing work and choosing replacement stone and doors. He employed the leading decorating firm Keeble and Co. of Carlisle Square in Soho, London, to execute the work and help find suitable antique doors and window and door frames for his desired restoration—Herbert Keeble himself seems to have

The 8th Earl scoured Europe to find suitable antique stone doorcases and oak doors to use in his restoration of the castle in the 1920s.

taken a lead role. They also helped reuse old things found in the castle; for instance, the red cloth that hangs in the staircase hall and makes such an effective backdrop for portraits was adapted from a set of existing bed hangings. The works were mostly complete by 1930, by which time bills from Keeble and Co. referred principally to furniture.[8]

Again collecting and decoration merge in this story, as they have done at Waddesdon Manor and at Arundel Castle, for Keeble acquired many things on the 8th Earl's behalf from dealers in London and Paris: furniture, fittings, stamped leather, and carved masonry details. These dealers included Jacques Seligman, Baci Frères, and Demotte, who shipped over carved armorials, which were then adapted to the coat of arms of the Berkeleys. Demotte supplied windows from the Chateau Charentonnay (in 1921 alone Demotte was paid some £3,774 9s 0d). Surviving accounts reveal that more than sixty windows in the castle were replaced with Gothic windows, which merge well with the historic structure.[9]

The Great Hall in particular was deliberately returned to a more convincing medieval appearance. A later ceiling was removed to reveal the original timber roof structure, and a huge fifteenth-century painted screen from Cefn Mably in Glamorganshire, which had belonged to the Kemeys-Tynte family, was introduced. As evidence of the 8th Earl's attention to detail, the screen was tried out here in a full-scale model before it was installed.

The survivals of the past were readily adapted to the needs of the present.

A view from the Great Hall towards the great painted screen. The 8th Earl revealed the original timber ceiling and had stained glass armorials commissioned for the windows.

The old screen from Cefn Mably was preserved but the Berkeley arms were painted in. A richly carved stone porch with old carved doors and fine figurative carving was imported from France (the doors are thought to come from Château de Chenaze) and added to the porch. The finely carved fifteenth-century chimneypiece in the Great Hall came from nearby Wanswell Court. The 8th Earl restored the original twelfth-century chapel at the suggestion of his American wife, who had been involved in chapel restorations in Italy.

The 8th Earl decided to convert the later chapel into the atmospheric Morning Room, with its ceiling timbers painted in red and green. The original colour scheme was somewhat restored. He introduced the carved and hooded chimneypiece and hung the room in Brussels tapestry. The oak screen from the chapel (which had originally come from Longridge Priory, Gloucestershire) was now moved to the Long Drawing Room, from which he in turn removed early-nineteenth-century panelling, although he preserved in this room an extensive suite of eighteenth-century giltwood furniture with petit-point embroidery by Elizabeth Drax.[10]

Keeble & Co. created handsome new rooms in 1922–28, ingeniously contriving comfortable and warm bedrooms and bathrooms in a style fitting for one of the oldest of English castles. Antique leather hangings were introduced into many of the bedrooms, and old screens and doors were adapted to create fitted wardrobes and washrooms. One bathroom lined in marble was bought from the Waldorf Astoria in New York.[11]

To furnish these rooms, the 8th Earl added to inherited pieces of furniture, acquiring a considerable amount of English and continental oak furniture.

The sixteenth-century textile on the wall of the staircase hall was originally a bed hanging found in the castle during the restoration and reused as a wall hanging, as part of an effort to build up suitable colours and textures.

above left A view into Drake's Bedroom, typical of the carefully furnished bedrooms of the castle, with four-poster oak beds

above right The marble-lined bathroom acquired from the Waldorf Astoria and inserted by the 8th Earl

In the Small Drawing Room, the vast and ancient timbers had been long plastered over before the 8th Earl stripped the plaster away to reveal them.

He created consistent, and comfortable, connoisseur-ly interiors as exemplified in "Drake's Bedroom," where reputedly Sir Francis Drake used to stay. The main furnishing themes were enlivened with textiles and Middle Eastern glazed tiles.

Such artistic restorations had many parallels in these years, from the work of Colonel Lyell at Barrington Court in Somerset to that of Consuelo Vanderbilt, the former Duchess of Marlborough, at Crowhurst Place in Sussex, or Lady Baillie at Leeds Castle in Kent. Nor should the house at Bailiffscourt in Sussex be overlooked, where, beginning in 1927, the wealthy Guinness heir, 1st Lord Moyne, built a complete medieval manor house from scratch, using fragments of older houses, mullioned windows, carved ceilings, timber, and doors.[12]

One of the 8th Earl's greatest pleasures at Berkeley Castle was adapting objects to provide electric lamps, including old silver candelabra and censers, as well as the gondola lamps in the Great Hall. This he did himself by hand. He was also, as James Miller has observed, "a man obsessed with the size of a corbel … [and] a champion of hot baths and even swimming pools."[13]

The Berkeleys provided generous hospitality to many visitors, and their friend Harold Hartley recalled, "Thanks to Lady Berkeley the jealously guarded privacy of Lord Berkeley's life relaxed, at least at the edges. The summer parties at Berkeley Castle, the stream of guests who passed through the house in Rome, found him a charming and considerate host even if they could not solve the enigma of his personality."

He also noted: "The romantic splendour of his surroundings was not an essential part of him, for he was above all a scientist; yet actually and historically it belonged to him, and seeing him against that background, those walls brown-pink like dried rose petals, it was hard to believe that the click of the calculating machine, breaking the silence of the courtyard, meant as much to him as the Castle that surrounded it."[14]

The work of the Earl and Countess of Berkeley was intended to recapture the beauty of the ancient castle, but was of course also a manifestation of its own time, a Romantic but aesthetically consistent programme of works that has its echoes in a number of architectural projects in the United States from the same years, such as Randolph Hearst's San Simeon. It remains a beloved family home to the Berkeley family today, inherited by a distant cousin of the 8th and last Earl, whose son and grandson live there still and preserve the 8th Earl's vision. The house and gardens are now open to the public.

The former chapel was transformed into the Morning Room by the removal of an oak screen and the insertion of a Gothic chimneypiece. The antique furniture and tapestries all contribute to an aesthetic interior.

15 PARHAM HOUSE

The Cult of the Manor House

PARHAM IN SUSSEX IS A HANDSOME, STONE-BUILT ELIZABETHAN house, but it is also one of the finest surviving examples of that early-twentieth-century and interwar phenomenon of the cherished manor house restoration. Mark Girouard wrote in *Life in the English Country House* (1978) that "if one had been looking for the typical country house of the first thirty years of this [the twentieth] century … the most likely candidate would have been neither an altogether new or an altogether old house, but an old house rescued from decay, lovingly restored and carefully enlarged and surrounded by new gardens."[1] It is interesting to note that Chequers, the official country retreat of

The embroidered flame-stitch hangings of the bed in the Great Chamber of Parham House. The coverlet, headboard, and tester are of 1580s French or Italian origin, associated with the circle of Marie de Medici.

233

The Great Hall was restored
over a number of decades in
the middle of the twentieth
century. The Pearsons
collected suitable portraits
and restored and lime-waxed
the panelling.

the British Prime Ministers, is just this sort of house also. After their marriage in 1915, the Hon. Clive Pearson (1887–1965) and his wife, Alicia Knatchbull-Hugessen, daughter of the 1st Lord Brabourne, bought Parham House and its estate for £200,000. The house was restored with the minutest care, and furnished and decorated with equal care. Pearson came from one of the great entrepreneurial families of the turn of the century. He was the younger son of Weetman Pearson, 1st Viscount Cowdray, and worked with his father and brother in the family engineering firm, the Pearson Corporation, which specialised in building railway tunnels in New York and Mexico, as well as in England.[2]

Parham House, Sussex, was acquired in 1922 by the Hon. Clive and Alicia Pearson, as a project to restore lovingly in the discerning spirit of the age.

From the start, the Pearsons wanted more than just a country house with a landed estate, although Clive Pearson certainly took great pleasure in fox hunting and land management alike. Both the Pearsons wanted a serious restoration project—this was to be the principal pastime of their married lives and a way for Clive Pearson to escape the demands of his busy career as an engineer. He and his wife had searched for an old house in need of loving care and found it at Parham, then sad and neglected. Pearson also brought his skill as an engineer to bear, and his wife was a serious historian. Their daughter, Veronica Tritton, recalled that her parents' passion was always for Elizabethan and Jacobean architecture: "in my childhood, grown-up conversations were filled with words like Littlecote, Loseley, Blickling, Danny, Wiston and many more."[3]

Their admiration for the older English manor house was something that belonged very much to their generation—an attitude that grew of the

In the Great Hall, a large equestrian portrait by Robert Peake of Henry, Prince of Wales, the eldest son of James I, hangs between a full-length portrait of Henry Howard, Earl of Surrey, and Robert Dudley, Earl of Leicester.

antiquarianism of the late eighteenth and early nineteenth centuries and the Gothic Revival of the mid-nineteenth century, a rejection of the Victorian historicism of styles imitated from the past. Added to this was a desire to celebrate the authentic beauty of old things, an attitude championed by Morris and connected to the Arts and Crafts enthusiasm for handcrafted building and furniture—a preference for oak over applied gilt furniture.

The distinct fashion for restoring older manor houses and furnishing them with well-chosen antiques and paintings could be seen at houses such as Great Dixter in Kent, restored and extended by Nathaniel Lloyd; Avebury Manor

and Great Chalfield Manor, both in Wiltshire; and Cothay Manor in Somerset. In some cases the taste for collecting old oak furniture even predated the purchase of a house of suitable period. Such houses in turn inspired the work of Arts and Crafts–inspired architects, from the Barnsleys to Lutyens.[4]

The Pearsons appointed Victor Heal as their architect. Heal had trained with the famous church architect G. F. Bodley, who had restored an old manor house at Water Eaton near Oxford for his own home. Heal embarked on the Parham restoration with meticulous attention to detail, and his work took a considerable amount of time. The Pearsons travelled a lot on business to South

The tall windows of the Great Hall face south, towards the Downs, and allow light to flood in. The original internal windows were uncovered in the 1930s.

The Pearsons also collected antique textiles, especially English needlework, and many fine examples are kept in the re-created Great Parlour.

America, so whenever Heal discovered an old door or window under plaster-work or behind panelling, all work had to be stopped until he and Pearson had exchanged cables and decided how best to proceed. Heal produced more than a thousand plans for the Pearsons, as well as albums of photographs and a scale model.[5]

Clive and Alicia Pearson did much of the necessary research themselves, with the help of a friend, Toby Wentworth-Fitzwilliam, who shared their love of antiquarian studies (and fox hunting). They filled fifty-three volumes with transcriptions of the Zouche family papers loaned by the Lady Zouche, who had sold Parham to Pearson. This is reminiscent of the eighteenth-century sporting gentlemen at Holkham returning from fox hunting to discuss classical literature, but for Pearson and his friend, old England was the Mount Olympus of the day.

The estate at Parham had originally been a monastic estate, belonging to the abbey of Westminister. It was granted to the Palmer family in 1540 and from 1601 was a possession of the Lords Zouche. The historical research was also continued by their daughter, Veronica Tritton. The information gleaned from their research influenced both architectural and decorative decisions. As Veronica Tritton recalled: "[Parham] history and how it grew also had to be discovered and so the Parham papers were constantly scanned for information

To perfect the interiors of Parham the Pearsons collected a wide range of suitable antique English furniture, including cabinets in lacquerwork and inlaid decoration, and antique musical instruments.

about the building, and in any architectural work that was done, every piece of evidence that was uncovered had to be considered."[6]

In general, the Pearsons' approach to the architecture and interior decoration of Parham was the same as the 8th Earl of Berkeley's at Berkeley Castle: to reveal the original character of the house and to complement it. Where there were problems, they resolved them with a view to the best result in overall aesthetic terms. The Pearsons were scholarly and sensitive; they were influenced by the aesthetic of authenticity that had evolved through the writings of Ruskin and Morris. The same approach can be traced in the lives and activities of Sir John and Lady Horner, who restored Mells Manor in Somerset in the 1880s, and Lord Curzon, who had taken a lease on Montacute and restored Bodiam Castle and Tattershall Castle, bequeathing both the latter to the National Trust.[7]

The Pearsons' ambition with the interiors at Parham was therefore both archaeological and aesthetic. They stripped away many later accretions to return the house to its Elizabethan glory. They restored and furnished every room in artistic, well-informed taste. For instance, all the original panelling in the house, which had been overpainted, was taken out, cleaned, repaired, and dry-waxed before being returned to the house.[8]

The furniture the Pearsons collected in the 1920s and '30s (and even in the 1950s) was of the best quality and chosen as either appropriate to the age and history of the house or to the character of each room. Some pieces were bought because they had associations with the families who had built or lived at Parham over the centuries, or because they told part of the story of the house, as with the portraits of Elizabeth and Robert Dudley, the Earl of Leicester. They also had a number of portraits relating to Alicia Pearson's family, the Knatchbull-Hugessens. Many of the paintings they collected are now recognised as of exceptional quality, including a rare allegorical portrait of Prince Henry, eldest son of James I.

The picture hang in the Great Hall, and the imaginative use of tapestries as curtains to the openings of the screens passage, are typical of the connoisseur-like approach, reflected in articles on country houses in magazines such as *Country Life* and in Percy MacQuoid's *Dictionary of English Furniture*, published in the 1920s. In fact, from the 1880s onwards a plethora of books was devoted to the study of old English architecture, paintings, and furniture, with beautifully taken pictures that people like the Pearsons could pore over and compare with their own. Like the *Country Life* photography of the time, the Pearsons and other collectors often arranged the rooms in a manner that suggests the elegance and comfort of the Dutch seventeenth-century paintings of domestic interiors.

The Great Parlour was re-created by the Pearsons, by the insertion of a new ceiling with plasterwork decoration by Esmond Burton, modelled by hand in the Arts and Crafts spirit, combining the crests, heraldic charges, and coats of arms of all the families who had owned Parham since it was built. They also introduced new panelling. In this room they concentrated early-seventeenth-century portraits of women, including Elizabeth of Bohemia, the strong colours of their clothes complemented by Mrs. Pearson's collection of gros-point and petit-point needlework furniture and tapestry, and carefully chosen carpets from the Middle East. In the neighbouring saloon, they decided to preserve the 1790s decoration that remained from Lord Zouche's remodelling

The saloon was preserved
by the Pearsons as a 1790s
drawing room interior,
as designed for the 12th
Lord Zouche. The painted
beechwood chair is
by Sheraton.

and to furnish the room in period style, including portraits by G. H. Harlow.[9]

On the staircase is a series of portraits connected with the Curzon family (the Lords Zouche), who owned the house from 1601 until it was sold to the Pearsons. The former Great Chamber was Mrs. Pearson's bedroom, with its Tudor bed, acquired from Wroxton Abbey in Oxfordshire, hung with an early-seventeenth-century flame-stitch pattern of around 1620. The flavour of a connoisseur's house is also felt in the West Room, where the Pearsons concentrated portraits and furniture of the later seventeenth century; the adjoining anteroom is hung in Hungarian needlework panels and on the floor is a rare example of an early needlework carpet.

The Long Gallery was the last of the rooms to be restored by the Pearsons, as late as the 1960s, and they sought the advice of Oliver Messel, the theatre designer whose family owned Nymans in Sussex, itself another manifestation of the early-twentieth-century taste for re-creating the atmosphere of a Tudor country house filled with plasterwork, tapestries, and oak furniture. The panelling in Parham's Long Gallery is all original but was lightened. The ceiling was altered in shape, and the sections between the oak ribs were painted with vinelike branches of oak leaves to Messel's designs, very much in the spirit of Elizabethan plaster decoration.[10]

After the Second World War, on the advice of their friend the art historian and collector Rupert Gunnis, the Pearsons opened the house to the public and

continued to improve and furnish with considered taste. This was quite a surprising decision for a shy couple who were more than sufficiently wealthy not to have to open their house for financial reasons.[11] Gunnis perhaps felt that they had put so much intelligent thought into the restoration and furnishing that it would help keep their commitment alive. This decision finds its parallel in a number of old manor houses that came to the National Trust, such as Great Chalfield Manor and Avebury Manor, both in Wiltshire. These loving restorations passed within the lifetime of the restorers to the trust because they were felt to express something important of the national character.

It could be said that the Pearsons made Parham and its interiors, in effect, a work of art. Its interiors are as carefully contrived and considered as any eighteenth-century house and capture the very essence of English country house taste of a certain generation, with a highly cultivated sense of history and comfort. Their vision has been maintained with great faithfulness by their daughter, Veronica Tritton, and more recently by their great-granddaughter, Lady Emma Barnard, and her husband, James.

The Green Room, a first-floor sitting room, is furnished with eighteenth-century pieces, and paintings and engravings associated with Sir Joseph Banks, a relation of Mrs. Pearson's family.

16 LIVING INTERIORS

The English Country House Interior Today

IN RECENT YEARS THERE HAS BEEN A CONSIDERABLE AMOUNT OF new work in the interiors of the English country house. This will have been already evident in the previous chapters, which show how much has been done in the past ten to twenty years just in the great houses featured in this book, often to achieve a balance between the key needs of comfort and display. Most of the principal programmes have been informed by a need to make sense of historic collections in houses that are still family homes, yet are also enjoyed by thousands of visiting public every year. But this recent activity belies the difficulties faced by country house owners in the middle years of the twentieth century.[1]

Ceramics by Edmund de Waal in the chapel corridor at Chatsworth, introduced by the 12th Duke of Devonshire, who moved into the house in 2006

The Garden Hall at Castle Howard in Yorkshire, decorated with imaginative paintings of Vanbrugh's architecture by Felix Kelly

If we take just the story of one of the country houses featured in this book, Castle Howard in Yorkshire, we can see the extraordinary crisis that faced so many houses in the middle of the twentieth century. A sharp rise in taxation, especially in death duties, aimed at undoing the political dominance of the landed class, inevitably and dramatically changed the finances available to maintain these historic country houses—reducing what could be spent on their maintenance and decoration, and even on the highly trained household staff that kept them in peak condition.

During the Second World War, most important country houses were turned over to military or institutional uses: the D-Day landings were planned in the Double Cube Room at Wilton (then the headquarters for Southern Command), Harewood House and Hatfield House were convalescent hospitals, and evacuees were fed by Baron Ferdinand Rothschild's chef at Waddeson Manor. Both Chatsworth and Castle Howard were used as girls' schools when children were evacuated from more vulnerable areas.

A fire at Castle Howard in November 1940, while the schoolchildren were in occupation, caused drastic damage. A large section of the south front on two floors was destroyed, as was the dome itself. George Howard (a grandson of the 9th Earl of Carlisle) inherited the house in his early twenties after the death of two older brothers in action—he himself was wounded in action in Burma. He returned from the war to find that the family's trustees were beginning to sell the contents, having decided that the family would never live in the house again. George Howard (later Lord Howard of Henderskelfe) took a different view, married Lady Cecilia Fitzroy, daughter of the 8th Duke of Grafton, moved into the house, and devoted his life to restoring the house and opening it to the public. He rebuilt the dome in 1960–62, thus recapturing the lost glory of Vanbrugh's original conception.[2]

During this generation many country houses were sold away from the

The library created in the 1980s for Lord Howard of Henderskelfe, designed in the Vanbrughian manner by architect Julian Bicknell

The Lady Cawdor Bedroom at Castle Howard is one of the new bedrooms restored in 2003 on the first floor, which had been destroyed in the 1940 fire and remained an empty void for more than sixty years.

estates or passed to the care of the National Trust. Some landowning families decided that the houses were too much of a burden to maintain as private houses. For the families that did continue in occupation, wartime austerity meant that materials were scarce and there was relatively little money to spend on improving or decorating country houses. Owners of houses in the 1950s and '60s often pursued a process of cautious custodianship and consolidation in taking care of the fabric of the house itself.

Howard, a chair of governors for the BBC, had his biggest break when, in the late 1970s, Granada TV decided to film the series *Brideshead Revisited*, based on the novel by Evelyn Waugh, with Jeremy Irons and Anthony Andrews, at Castle Howard. With funds from the project, George Howard refitted the Garden Hall, decorated with murals by Felix Kelly, and created a new library in 1983–84 in part of the burned-out shell of the central south front (both rooms were designed by young architect Julian Bicknell). The international success of the TV programme itself was part of the modern watershed in public popularity for the culture of the country house.

The story has become so identified with the house that the 2008 remake of the film used the house as a set once more. Lord Howard's son, the Hon. Simon Howard, has continued the process of restoration and in 2003 created bedrooms on the burned-out first floor, including Lady Cawdor's bedroom, suitable for guests but also open to visitors. In 2005 a drawing room was rehung in a turquoise blue silk damask woven in France, and a suite of John Linnell furniture (long in store) was restored and reupholstered. The carpet was designed and produced especially by Bamfords.

For the houses that remain in private ownership, Castle Howard's story is not unusual. The slow revival of country houses in the later twentieth century is a complex and interesting story with a number of different factors coming into play. The *Destruction of the Country House* exhibition held at the Victoria and Albert Museum in 1975, under the directorship of Sir Roy Strong, marked a watershed in public awareness of the losses: the collections dispersed, the historic country houses demolished, and the increasing cultural value of those that survive. The Gowers Report, drawn up in the late 1940s, had already referred to a cultural collapse the equivalent of the Dissolution of the Monasteries.[3]

Even in 1974 James Lees-Milne wrote that the country house was "as archaic as the osprey."[4] But since the mid-1970s public opinion has shifted sharply in favour of the protection of such an important element in the English story. Legal tax provisions have been introduced in exchange for public access to the great houses (especially to preserve collections intact). The Victoria and Albert Museum and the National Trust both help raise awareness and appreciation of historic furniture and design, as has the curatorial team of Temple Newsam House, Leeds, part of Leeds City Art Gallery, and others.

In 1985 *The Treasure Houses of Britain* at the National Gallery of Art in Washington, D.C., illustrated the consolidation of new interest in English country houses to an international audience.[5] During the same decade the National Trust acquired a series of important country houses—from Belton House, to Kedleston and Calke Abbey—and the restorations of these houses paralleled a renewed interest in the historic decoration of the country house. Among private owners, the example set by the 11th Duke and Duchess of Devonshire (the legendary "Debo") at Chatsworth is well known, having made the house comfortable for family use and public opening, with an unmistakable sense of style.

The Turquoise Drawing Room at Castle Howard: a newly woven damask was hung in 2005, and the Linnell seat furniture was restored and brought out from store.

There were key professional decorators in the 1950s who were helping both country house owners and the National Trust improve the quality of inherited interiors that were often, but not always, denuded of key pieces of art and furniture. John Fowler, in particular, worked on many of the great houses (including Wilton, Boughton, Waddesdon, and Syon featured in this book), but, perhaps not surprisingly, after fifty years little of his own work survives intact. One example is the warm colour scheme in the cloisters at Wilton, which has been preserved and restored, and another is the drawing room at Boughton for the 7th Duke and Duchess of Buccleuch in the late 1940s and '50s.[6]

Fowler worked with Sybil Colefax, and from this collaboration arose the firm Colefax and Fowler, the renowned purveyor of "the English Country House look." The company was co-owned by the talented and well-connected Virginian-born Nancy Lancaster, who had made her name decorating Ditchley Park in Oxfordshire and Kelmarsh Hall in Northamptonshire, of which she was successively chatelaine.[7] Lancaster was once accused of costing the English aristocracy a lot of money because she encouraged an expectation of comfort in bedrooms and bathrooms that had been forgotten in the years of austerity. Fowler stressed the importance of understanding the history of interior decoration and in 1974 cowrote *Interior Decoration of the Eighteenth Century* with John Cornforth of *Country Life* magazine, another important champion of the historic interior. Fowler was knowledgeable about historic decoration but in fact was often working towards a loosely artistic version of an authentic

Two views of the drawing room at Boughton House, Northamptonshire, a rare surviving example of the subtle, muted interior decoration employed by the great John Fowler during the 1950s

The new entrance hall at Goodwood, a room added to the private family side of the house by the present Earl and Countess of March to the designs of Christopher Smallwood Architects

original in the interests of making a room work for a new generation.[8]

In the years of austerity, Fowler was remarkably inventive and, for instance, reused old curtains as upholstery. Like so many of the best decorators, Fowler was sympathetic to people actually living in historic interiors. In the words of Deborah Devonshire, even in his most controversial work at Sudbury Hall, Derbyshire, "unwelcoming cold rooms [were] turned into a fairyland under his direction."[9]

Other great names of this world include David Hicks. Although his name was usually associated with high-profile London projects, his work in country houses was much admired (such as Baronscourt in Ireland). Hicks championed a more modernist-inspired use of bolder colours and strong patterns that had considerable influence on a succeeding generation of decorators. More recently, historic paint experts such as Ian Bristow and Patrick Baty have developed a scientific analysis of paint, meaning that new projects can be fully informed as to original schemes before decisions are made about colour and paint technique. (Patrick Baty advised on Wilton, Syon, Waddesdon, and Goodwood in this book.)

David Mlinaric, the current doyen of the country house interior decorating world who began his career in the 1950s and has worked on many of the important houses featured in this book, recalls how often in the 1950s and '60s budgets were tight and owners would work on one room at a time, just

The Small Drawing Room at Arundel Castle, redecorated in the 1990s by the present Duchess of Norfolk, with advice from David Mlinaric, incorporating the Canaletto paintings from Park House

One of the family's private rooms, the library at Wilton House, Wiltshire, was decorated by Rex Whistler in the 1930s. The wallpaper was introduced by John Fowler in the 1960s, while the bookshelves have been recently reintroduced.

changing paint colours and curtains. This inevitably restricted the palette as decorators "had to choose colours that would work with untouched interiors in neighbouring rooms. It was twenty years before I was asked to do any new gilding." He recalls that while trying to balance a new colour scheme to an old and faded one in the 1950s, one of the professional painters said, "I can't match dirt, David!"[10]

Typical of the great country houses whose interiors have undergone a major recent revival, thanks in part to a preceding period of repair to the fabric of the house, is Goodwood House in Sussex. The 9th Duke of Richmond, as chairman of the Goodwood Group of Companies from 1961, had overseen a long programme of consolidation. Part of the house behind the main Wyatt ranges was demolished in the 1960s, but the main Wyatt building and the Palladian interiors by Morris and Brettingham were retained and repaired.

The Duke's eldest son, Charles, Earl of March, and his wife, moved into the main house in 1994 and began the revival of the interiors (including many of the rooms featured in chapter 10), with advice from Lady Victoria Waymouth on interior decoration, Alec Cobbe on the hanging of pictures, and Christopher Smallwood Architects on the architecture. Former curator Rosemary Baird, who provided the background research and other advice, recalls: "in many ways, Goodwood had lost its Regency character. We worked to bring

overleaf *The drawing room in the east wing of Arundel Castle, the private family room of the house, where strong colours and bold furniture have brought style and comfort to the Gothic revival interior*

The dining room at Wilton House, a neo-Caroline room created in the early twentieth century but long used for other purposes, was restored and refurnished in 2010 by the present Earl and Countess of Pembroke, with advice from David Mlinaric.

back the verve and strong colours of the date and to reflect the taste of the Earl and Countess of March without making free with history."[11] The family today occupies the rooms that were historically considered the private apartments. A new entrance hall to these rooms was added in 2005 to help resolve a gap in circulation left by the demolitions of the 1960s. It was designed by Christopher Smallwood Architects and shows how a contemporary classical interior could help make a country house work more comfortably for a family, while providing a suitable space for the display of historic contents. Lord March hopes that the new hall, as with all the recent works to the house, adds to the historic ensemble: "I need to feel that we are pressing forward and making changes that are relevant to today—creating a future from the very best of the past."[12]

In the same county, Arundel Castle was also reoccupied fully as a family home by a new generation. In 1960 the 16th Duke of Norfolk moved into a new house in the park, Park House, designed by Claude Phillimore. When he died in 1975, Arundel Castle was inherited by his cousin, the 17th Duke, who did not move into the castle but set up a dedicated trust to look after it—one of the first of its kind.[13] In 1987 his son and heir, Edward (then the Earl of Arundel), married Georgina Gore, and they decided to live in the east wing. This was in fact the original family wing at Arundel Castle, where the 15th Duke had lived while surpervising his great works. The Countess of Arundel

furnished it with style, with advice from David Mlinaric and others, using strong, warm colours, rich textiles, and furniture brought out from store.

The overall impact of this work, informed by historical research and understanding provided by John Martin Robinson, has hugely improved the feeling and flavour of this remarkable house, and works continue to the gardens and estate. Mlinaric recalls, "The palette needed to be much stronger there as the architecture is quite powerful."[14] The private apartments of the east wing were redecorated between 1987 and 1989 (with Vernon Gibberd as architect and Mlinaric advising on the interiors). The library was restored at the same time, and in the mid-1990s the larger bedroom suites in the main castle range were also redecorated, advised by Mlinaric and later Edward Bulmer. In 2000 the Small Drawing Room was given a new colour scheme by Mlinaric to accommodate Canaletto paintings that had been returned to the castle after the death of Lavinia, Duchess of Norfolk. The redecoration of the magnificent

Large Drawing Room, on which Robert Kime advised, was completed in 2007.

In 2003 the present (18th) Earl of Pembroke inherited Wilton House at the age of twenty-five. As in other houses, his father, a film director, had concentrated on repairing the fabric and the roof. Trained in industrial design and now married to an interior decorator, the 18th Earl has been responsible for a major sequence of re-presentation of the historic interiors. This has been built on the example and stewardship of his late father and on advice from such experts as historian John Martin Robinson and David Mlinaric. The classical sculpture around the house and gardens has been moved back into the cloisters, where it was originally displayed (but moved out after a sale in the 1960s).[15] The final element of the redecoration is what had long been the family ping-pong room. Initiated by the present Countess of Pembroke, this room, which had been designed as a grand dining room in the first decade of the twentieth century, was returned to a vibrant dark and green-blue colour scheme unveiled in 2010. The caryatids of the doorcase were created by Stephen Pettifer, a craftsman based at Wilton who also copied a historic chandelier so that a pair could be hung over the table. Tapestries, paintings, and furniture were brought in from around the house and from store. Lord Pembroke recalls: "It took nearly two years, but when you do something for a house such as Wilton, you want it to be able to last 200."[16]

Another of the great houses featured in this book, Hatfield House in Hertfordshire has been home to the Cecil family for more than four hundred years. It has been subject to a series of revived and newly presented interiors since 2003, when the house and estate were taken over by the current (7th) Marquess and Marchioness of Salisbury. Many subtle improvements to the presentation of the house have been made, foremost of which is perhaps the rehang of the picture collection in the King James Drawing Room, with advice from Alec Cobbe. The paintings are hung over Brussels tapestry to brilliant effect that evokes the colour and glamour of the English country house tradition.

With an eye to ensuring that a contribution of the new generation includes new art commissions, Lord Salisbury also has a new desk inlaid with hunting scenes, commissioned from cabinetmaker Rupert Browne. Browne also designed and made the gilded Chinese dragons, which are part of the new chinoiserie scheme in the bedroom that adjoins the King James Drawing Room. This crowns a canopied structure that ingeniously conceals a bathroom for this bedroom while adding visual interest for any visitor. Other work was by the estate's own team of in-house craftsmen led by Anthony Downes. Lord Salisbury remarks: "We cannot really alter or rebuild on a big scale but what we can do as successors is to make our contribution and improve the comfort and aesthetics of the place. These houses are not institutions but still lived in and each generation keeps them alive and builds on the existing patina."[17]

The aforementioned work undertaken by the 11th Duke and Duchess of Devonshire ("Debo") at Chatsworth in Derbyshire is a revival that has undoubtedly contributed to the national profile of the historic country house. Their son and his wife, the present (12th) Duke and Duchess, who moved into the house in January 2006, have continued to build on this foundation. As well as works undertaken to the state apartment already featured, they have in the past year unveiled three new galleries on the second storey of Chatsworth. Two were originally the Sketch Galleries that displayed the 6th Duke's collection of Old Master drawings. These were reordered to create distinct rooms with their

The redecoration and re-presentation of the Sketch Galleries at Chatsworth for the present Duke and Duchess of Devonshire include one room (the South Sketch Gallery, top left and bottom right) devoted to furniture and paintings associated with the legendary Duchess Georgiana, including her mineral collection, and another (the North Sketch Gallery, top right and bottom left), devoted to the modern art and furniture collected by the Duke and Duchess and the Duke's parents.

own strong identities, under the advice of architect Peter Inskip, interior decorator David Mlinaric, and furniture expert Jonathan Bourne, who also worked on the state apartment together. A third, contemporary gallery was created on the north side out of former bedrooms, bathrooms, and service rooms. In the South Sketch Gallery, for instance, windows have been opened up, new chimneypieces have been inserted, and, on the advice of Mlinaric, the room was hung in a French pale green striped moiré and the windows hung with elegant curtains. A series of portraits, furniture, and objects in this gallery tell the story of the famous eighteenth-century Duchess Georgiana.

The adjoining West Sketch Gallery has been furnished and hung to display portraits, Old Master paintings, and William Kent furniture associated with the Burlington inheritance, which came to Chatsworth through the marriage of the 5th Duke's father to the only surviving daughter of Richard Boyle, the Palladian champion, the 3rd Earl of Burlington. The two galleries are united by a colour scheme, but in the West Sketch Gallery there is a plain moiré on the walls.

A third gallery has been created by Peter Inskip on the north side of the central courtyard and again follows the essential colour scheme of the two sketch galleries but is hung in plain cloth. Here are displayed modern works of art from the collections formed by the present Duke and his wife, Amanda, and by the Duke's parents, ranging from works by Lucian Freud to a recent digital portrait by Michael Craig-Martin of Laura, the present Countess of

The minerals and smaller antiquities rearranged in the Chapel Corridor at Chatsworth to impressive visual effect with advice from Jonathan Bourne

Burlington, wife of the Duke's son. This is a very welcome attempt to show contemporary art hung in the character of an elegant domestic interior, part of a continuing story of connoisseurship and enjoyment of art, and another example of what has been dubbed "ducal chic."[19]

It is always possible to add. Lord Rothschild inherited the Waddesdon Manor estates in 1988, and with this came the management role for the house, which had been vested in the National Trust. Lord Rothschild put his energies into a major centenary campaign of renewal and redecoration. His design team included both the interior decorator David Mlinaric and the architect Peter Inskip. Described as a modern incarnation of *le style Rothschild*, the work included the new state rooms on the first floor, and the smoking room, billiard room, and a series of bedrooms that make up the bachelor's wing. The Blue Dining Room was fitted with mid-eighteenth-century boiserie panelling, originally from the Hôtel Thiroux Paris, which had been bought by Baron Ferdinand Rothschild for his London house and stored in the estate yard here for many years.[20]

These boiseries were restored by specialists in France and painted in situ to an eighteenth-century recipe, following the original blue found on the panels. Two of the walls were hung in a matching blue silk damask woven in Tours to an original eighteenth-century pattern, framed in a white gold fillet that reads as silver but does not tarnish. The curtains were made from the same damask.

Lord Rothschild and the National Trust are keen to incorporate new works of art that help guests and visitors look at the magnificence of Waddesdon Manor in new and interesting ways as well as reinforce the sense that the house is more than just a great museum. With this in mind, a chandelier was commissioned for this room in 2003 made of broken crockery and cutlery by Ingo Maurier. The striking chairs and chandelier shown in the photograph of the Blue Dining Room are by Brazilian designers Fernando and Humberto Campana and are on temporary display in 2010. They capture a zany sense of Baroque theatricality in their form and colour and say something of the determination and courage that lies behind all the new works at Waddesdon Manor—and the ways in which new works can be seen alongside the old.

This book on English country house interiors looks at the subject through the example of fourteen great country houses chosen for their period qualities. This survey of recent works is illustrative and is by nature only a partial account (for there are other great houses we might have featured, including others cared for by the National Trust). But these houses, with interiors rooted in a subtle balance of comfort, prestige, and display, all have an important place in English history and culture. The public opening of these houses over the past half a century has changed the way in which such houses are seen and enjoyed. The 11th Duke of Devonshire once said, "it is one of the greatest pleasures in the world, to share with others the things you are lucky enough to have."[21]

The general level of appreciation of the quality of furniture and art encountered in these houses has perhaps reached a settled level—fifty years ago they were not valued so highly. The quality of the presentation of these great rooms, and the interest in these rooms being living interiors with their own story of continuity, has affected the way in which such interiors are perceived and enjoyed. The changes in interior decoration and presentation in the past twenty years—even in the past five—show that even in the historic environment, nothing remains quite still. And yet the past is always present.

ACKNOWLEDGEMENTS

Any book involves so many hands; this book was first suggested to me by David Morton when we first met after a lecture at the Colony Club, and the idea developed with Charles Miers and Alexandra Tart. It has been a pleasure to have worked with them all on this and I appreciate their guidance, experience, and confidence in the subject—especially Alexandra Tart's wise and tactful editing. The opportunity to work closely on this project with Paul Barker, whom I have known since 1995, was a privilege indeed and has resulted in I believe an unrivalled survey of some of the great country house interiors to survive. Paul is patient and thorough and has a feeling for these houses and the way light falls in them. I could hardly imagine a better designer to pull all these things together than Robert Dalrymple, who has approached the book with sensitivity and good sense and has been a pleasure to work with.

This book would simply not have been possible without the support of the owners and trustees responsible for these houses featured, and the curatorial and administrative teams of each of the houses. I should like to thank especially the Marquis and Marchioness of Salisbury, Robin Harcourt Williams, Nick Moorhouse, and Shana Fleming at Hatfield House; the Earl and Countess of Pembroke, Chris Rolfe, Sarah King, Charlotte Spender, and Nigel Bailey at Wilton; the Duke and Duchess of Buccleuch, Charles Lister, Gareth Fitzpatrick, and Michael Crick at Boughton; the Duke and Duchess of Devonshire, Matthew Hirst, Hannah Obee, Charles Noble, Diane Naylor, and Mollie Moseley at Chatsworth; the Hon. Mr. and Mrs. Simon Howard, Christopher Ridgway, and Ann Louise Mason at Castle Howard; the Marquis and Marchioness of Cholmondley, John Marchant, and Susan Cleaver at Houghton; Viscount and Viscountess Coke, the Earl and Countess of Leicester, Colin Shearer at Holkham Hall; the Earl and Countess of Lascelles, Anna Robinson, Pauline Chandler, and Aimee Rawson at Harewood House; the Duke and Duchess of Northumberland and Lisa Little at Syon; the Earl and Countess of March, James Peill, and Rosemary Baird at Goodwood; the Duke and Duchess of Norfolk, John Martin Robinson, Bryan McDonald, and Sara Rodger at Arundel Castle; Lord Rothschild, Pippa Shirley, Diana Stone, and the National Trust at Waddesdon Manor; Mr. and Mrs. Charles Berkeley and Mr. and Mrs. John Berkeley and David Wintle at Berkeley Castle; James and Lady Emma Barnard and Richard Pailthorpe at Parham House.

My understanding for country house interiors was I think probably inspired from a young age by my mother Elizabeth's creativity and interest in the arts, my grandmother Bunty's innate good taste and ability to take pleasure in fine things, and my father Roger's annual cricket match at Petworth House (I recall him saying: "shall we go and see the Turner's?"). My art master at Winchester, the late Graham Drew, encouraged me to use my eyes, and Nigel McGilchrist, who ran a course on art history and Italian culture at the Anglo-Italian Institute in Rome, housed then in a building designed by Piranesi, taught me to see things in a European context. At the Warburg Institute, I studied art, iconography, and classical literature and philosophy under Michael Baxandall and Charles Hope; and at the Victorian Society I was further inspired by the knowledge and enthusiasm of Teresa Sladen, Gavin Stamp, Andrew Saint, and many others.

Working for the National Trust I was privileged to know and work with some of the most talented house curators and experts, including Martin Drury and Gervase Jackson-Stops, and I learnt especially from Merlin Waterson, David Adshead, Julie Marsden, Helen Lloyd, Anthea Palmer, Jonathan Marsden, Julian Gibbs, John Maddison, and John Sutcliffe. It was at the National Trust where I first worked with the late John Cornforth, the doyen of scholars of the interiors of country houses, and I am indebted to him for so much. I joined *Country Life* in 1995 under Clive Aslet as editor, who sent me all over the British Isles in search of the best and most beautiful houses, and Michael Hall, as architectural editor, to whom I am particularly indebted for his encouragement and guidance over so many years; I continued to learn so much from all the former and regular contributors whom it then became my privilege to edit: Marcus Binney, Mark Girouard, John Goodall, Giles Worsley, Ian Gow, John Martin Robinson, Richard Haslam, Antony Woodward, William Palin, Christopher Woodward, Mary Miers, and many others, every one bringing their own knowledge and passion to the wonderful cocktail of *Country Life* and its weekly articles on country houses. Indeed, all my colleagues at *Country Life* have helped shape my views over the years, including Rupert Uloth, Mark Hedges, Anne Wright, Octavia Pollock, Polly Chiappetta, Phil Crewdson, and Camilla Costello.

I am also grateful to the history of art undergraduates whom I supervised at Cambridge in the 2007–08 academic year for the opportunity to discuss such things with bright young minds and the scholars of the Attingham Summer School whom I lecture and meet every year also for their stimulating questions and opinions.

For this book I am especially indebted to John Hardy, who has encouraged it from the start and advised on my texts with a great generosity of spirit, and even came to Boughton to arrange a tea service for one photograph; Leslie Geddes-Brown, who likewise has read all the text with great kindness and sagacity, as did Tessa Murdoch of the V&A. Inevitably I am very grateful to writers and scholars and friends who have influenced my views and informed my understanding of architectural and decorative history, including Sir Roy Strong, David Mlinaric, Alec Cobbe, John Martin Robinson, David Watkin, Tim Mowl, Ptolemy Dean, Simon Thurley, Anna Keay, Ben Pentreath, John and Eileen Harris, Rosemary Baird, Christopher Ridgway, Matthew Hirst, Lucy Worsley, Frank Salmon, Harriet Salisbury, Georgiana Campbell, Desmond and Penny Guinness, Rupert Thomas, Tim Knox, Charles Cator, and the Dowager Duchess of Devonshire, as well as others mentioned in the endnotes and bibliography and all those owners and curators named above who gave me time and looked over the texts as they were being completed. I am also indebted to wise and kind librarians at the University of Cambridge Library, the London Library, and the British Library.

Finally, my deepest thanks to my wife, Sophie, who has a brilliant eye and an understanding of the decorative arts which she herself studied to post-graduate level, and to our two beautiful daughters, Georgia and Miranda, who continue to delight their parents in every way, for their patience with the time away from them that has to be devoted to a book such as this—and to my Jack Russell, Archie, my most constant companion in the writing "shed" in my Cambridge garden.

Paul Barker would like to stress his thanks to all those who helped his visits to the houses who have been mentioned above. He especially thanks his wife, Tracy, without whom such a book could not look as good as it does; and his son George, who he hopes will enjoy looking at it and reading it one day.

BIBLIOGRAPHY

Adam, James, and Robert Adam. *Works in Architecture*, vol. 1. New York: Dover Publications Inc., reprinted 1980.

Aldrich, Megan, ed. *The Craces: Royal Decorators, 1768–1899*. London: John Murray, 1990.

Aldrich, Megan. *Gothic Revival*. Oxford: Phaidon, 1997.

Angelicoussis, Elizabeth. *The Holkham Collection of Classical Sculptures*. Mainz am Rheim: Von Zabern, 2001.

Aslet, Clive. *The Last Country Houses*. New Haven and London: Yale University Press, 1982.

Baird, Rosemary. *Goodwood: Art, Architecture, Sport and Family*. London: Frances Lincoln, 2007.

Baird, Rosemary. "Goodwood House, Sussex." *Country Life* (24 July 1997): 44–51.

———. "The Refurbishment of the State Rooms at Goodwood House." *Apollo* (January 1997): 3–5.

Barbet, Jean. *Livre d'Architecture d'Autels et de Cheminees*, 1632.

Barker, Nicolas. *The Devonshire Inheritance: Five Centuries of Collections at Chatsworth*. Alexandria, VA: Art Services International, 2003.

Barnard, Lady Emma, et al. *Parham, West Sussex Guidebook*. Heritage House, Wymondham, 2010.

Beard, Geoffrey. *Craftsmen and Interior Decoration in England, 1660–1820*. New York: Holmes and Meier, 1981.

———. *Stucco and Decorative Plasterwork in Europe*. London: Thames and Hudson, 1983.

———. *The Work of John Vanbrugh*. London: Batsford, 1986.

Berkeley, John, and Vita Sackville-West. *Berkeley Guide Book*. Ketteringham, Norfolk: Heritage House Media, 2009.

Berkeley, Molly. *Beaded Bubbles*. London: H. Hamilton, 1967.

Blakesley, Rosalind. *The Arts and Crafts Movement*. London: Phaidon, 2006.

Bold, John. *Wilton House and English Palladianism*. London: HMSO, 1988.

Bristow, Alan. *Interior House-Painting Colours and Technology, 1615–1840*. New Haven and London: Yale University Press, 1996.

Buccleuch, The Duke of, Charles Lister and Gareth Fitzpatrick. *Boughton*. Derby: Heritage House Group, 2006.

Calloway, Stephen, ed. *The Elements of Style*, 2nd ed. London: Mitchell Beazley, 1996.

Campbell, Colin. *Vitruvius Britannicus*. New York: Dover Publications, 2006.

Cecil, Lord David. *The Cecils of Hatfield House*. London: Constable, 1973.

Chalcraft, Anna. *Strawberry Hill*. London: Frances Lincoln, 2007.

Chippendale, Thomas. *The Gentleman and Cabinet-Maker's Director*, a reprint of the third edition. Dover: Dover Publications Inc., 1966.

Clark, Kenneth. *The Gothic Revival*. London: John Murray, 1962.

Colvin, Howard. *A Biographical Dictionary of British Architects, 1600–1840*, 4th edition. London: Paul Mellon Centre, 2008.

Cooper, Nicholas. *The Jacobean Country House*. London: Aurum, 2006.

Cornforth, John. *Early Eighteenth Century Interior Decoration*. New Haven and London: Yale University Press, 2004.

———. *English Interiors 1790–1848: The Quest for Comfort*. London: Barrie and Jenkins, 1978.

———. *Houghton Hall*. Derby: Heritage House Group, 2007.

———. *The Inspiration of the Past*. London: Viking, 1985.

———. "Parham Park Revisited." *Country Life* 177 (June 6, 1985): 1566–70 and (June 13, 1985): 1658–62.

———. *The Search for a Style: Country Life and Architecture, 1897–1935*. London and New York: W.W. Norton & Co., 1988.

———. "Waddesdon Manor." *Country Life* (June 8, 1995): 122–27.

Cornforth, John, and John Fowler. *Eighteenth Century Interior Decoration*. London: Barrie and Jenkins, 1978.

Cornforth, John, and Oliver Hill. *English Country Houses: Caroline, 1625–85*. London: Country Life, 1985.

Croft, Pauline. "Cecil Robert, First Earl of Salisbury (1563–1612)." In *Oxford Dictionary of National Biography*, edited by H.C.G. Matthew and Brian Harrison, vol. 10. Oxford and New York: Oxford University Press, 2004.

Croft-Murray, Edward. *Decorative Painting in England 1537–1837*, 2 vols. London: Country Life, 1962.

Cook, Olive. *The English Country House: An Art and a Way of Life*. London and New York: W. W. Norton & Co., 1984.

Cunningham, Peter, ed. *The Letters of Horace Walpole*, 9 vols. Edinburgh: John Grant, 1906.

de Rothschild, Mrs. James. *The Rothschilds at Waddesdon Manor*. London: Collins, 1979.

Devonshire, The Duchess of. "The Full Blown Country-House Look." *The Spectator* 15 (December 2007): 84.

———. *The House: A Portrait of Chatsworth*. London: Macmillan, 1982.

Duncan-Jones, Katherine. *Sir Philip Sidney: Courtier Poet*. London: Hamish Hamilton, 1991.

Esterly, David. *Grinling Gibbons and the Art of Carving*. London: Victoria and Albert Museum, 1998.

Ferguson, Niall. *The World's Banker: The History of the House of Rothschild*. London: Weidenfeld and Nicolson, 1998.

Fowler, Claire. *Chatsworth*. Bakewell: Chatsworth House Trust, 2010.

Garnett, Oliver. *Living in Style: A Guide to Historic Decoration and Ornament*. London: National Trust, 2002.

Claire Gapper, John Newman, and Annabel Ricketts. "Hatfield: A House for a Lord Treasurer." In *Patronage, Culture and Power: The Early Cecils*, edited by Pauline Croft. New Haven and London: Yale University Press, 2002.

Gore, Alan, and Ann Gore. *The History of English Interiors*. Oxford: Phaidon, 1991.

Girouard, Mark. *Life in the English Country House*. London: Yale University Press, 1978.

———. *The Victorian Country House*. New Haven and London: Yale University Press, 1979.

Gowers, Sir Ernest. *The Gowers Report on Outstanding Historical or Architectural Interest*. London: HMSO, 1950.

Guinness, Desmond. *The Palladian Style in England, Ireland and America*. London: Thames & Hudson, 1974.

Hall, Michael. *The Victorian Country House*. London: Aurum, 2009.

———. *Waddesdon Manor: The Heritage of a Rothschild House*. New York: Abrams, in association with Waddesdon Manor, 2002.

Hardy, John. "The Interiors." In *Holkham Hall*, edited by Leo Schmidt, et al. London and Munich: Prestel, 2005.

Harewood, The Earl of. *Harewood*, revised ed. Leeds: Harewood House Trust, 2009.

Harris, Eileen. *The Country Houses of Robert Adam*. London: Aurum, 2007.

———. *The Genius of Robert Adam: His Interiors*. New Haven and London: Yale University Press, 2001.

Harris, John. *Moving Rooms*. New Haven and London: Yale University Press, 2007.

Hart, Vaughan. *Sir John Vanbrugh: Storyteller in Stone*. New Haven and London: Yale University Press, 2008.

Hart, Vaughan. *Nicholas Hawksmoor: Rebuilding Ancient Wonders*. New Haven and London: Yale University Press, 2002.

Hartley, Harold. "Randal Thomas Mowbray Rawdon Berkeley, Earl of Berkeley." *Journal of the Royal Society* (1942): 167–82.

Hatfield Guidebook. Norwich: Jarrold, 2007.

Hill, Rosemary. *God's Architect: Pugin and the Building of Romantic Britain*. London: John Murray, 2007.

Honour, Hugh. *Chinoiserie*. London: John Murray, 1961.

Honour, Hugh, and Fleming, John, (eds.) *The Penguin Dictionary of Decorative Arts*. London: Allen Lane/Penguin, 1977.

Hosford, David. "Cavendish, William, 1st Duke of Devonshire." In *Oxford Dictionary of National Biography*, edited by H.C.G. Matthew and Brian Harrison, 664–71, 1641–1707. Oxford and New York: Oxford University Press, 2004.

Howard, Maurice. *The Early Tudor Country House*. London: George Philip, 1987.

Hughes, Helen, ed. *John Fowler: The Invention of Country House Style*. Donhead St. Mary: Donhead, 2005.

Hussey, Christopher. "Berkeley Castle, Gloucestershire." *Country Life* (December 15, 1955), 1430–33.

———. *English Country Houses: Early Georgian 1715–1760*. London: Country Life, 1955.

Jackson, Anna. *The V&A Guide to Period Style: 400 Years of British Art and Design*. London: V&A Publishing, 2002.

Jackson-Stops, Gervase. "French and Dutch Influence on Architecture and Interiors." In *Boughton House: The English Versailles*, edited by Tessa Murdoch, 56–65. London: Faber and Faber/Christies, 1992.

Jackson-Stops, Gervase, ed. *The Treasure Houses of Britain*, exhibition catalogue. National Gallery of Art, Washington, D.C. New Haven and London: Yale University Press, 1985.

Jacques, Dennett. *A Visit to Goodwood*. Chichester: Dennett Jacques, 1822.

Jenkins, Simon. *England's Thousand Best Houses*. London: Allen Lane/Penguin, 2003

King, David. *The Complete Works of Robert and James Adam*. London: Butterworth, 1991.

Kirk, Jayne. *Parham: An Elizabethan House and Its Restoration*. Chichester: Phillimore, 2009.

Lancaster, Osbert. *Here of All Places*. London: John Murray, 1959.

Lawson Dick, Oliver, ed. *Aubrey's Brief Lives*. London: Penguin, 1982.

Lees-Milne, James. *Earls of Creation*. London: Hamish Hamilton, 1962.

———. *English Country House Baroque, 1685–1715*. London: Country Life, 1970.

Leicester, The Earl of, et al. *Holkham*. Great Ellingham: Arie and Ingrams, 2004.

McQuorquodale, Charles. *The History of Interior Decoration*. Oxford: Phaidon, 1983.

Messel, Thomas, ed. *Oliver Messel: In the Theatre of Design*. New York: Rizzoli International Publications, 2011.

Metzer, Edward. "Montagu, Ralph, First Duke of Montagu." In *Oxford Dictionary of National Biography*, edited by H.C.G. Matthew and Brian Harrison, vol. 38, 760–62. Oxford and New York: Oxford University Press, 2004.

Miers, Mary. *The English Country House*. New York: Rizzoli International Publications, 2009.

Miller, James. "Berkeley Castle." *Country Life* (December 2, 2004): 70–75; and (December 5, 2004): 56–61.

———. *Hidden Treasure Houses*. London: Macmillan, 2006.

Mlinaric, David, and Mirabel Cecil. *Mlinaric on Decorating*. London: Frances Lincoln 2008.

Montgomery-Massingberd, Hugh. *Great Houses of England and Wales*. London: Laurence King, 2000.

Morris, Christopher, ed. *The Illustrated Journeys of Celia Fiennes, c.1682–c.1712*. London: Macmillan, 1988.

Mowl, Tim. *William Kent: Architect, Designer and Opportunist*. London: Pimlico, 2007.

Murdoch, Tessa, ed. *Boughton House: The English Versailles*. London: Faber and Faber/Christies, 1992.

———. *Noble Households: Eighteenth-Century Inventories of Great English Houses*. Cambridge: Adamson, 2006.

Musson, Jeremy. "Chatsworth, Derbyshire." *Country Life* 102, no. 12 (March 12, 2007): 86–91.

———. *The English Manor House*. London: Aurum, 1999.

———. *In Pursuit of Antiquity: Drawings from the Giants of British Neo-classicism*. London: Sir John Soane's Museum, 2010.

———. *Plasterwork*. London: Aurum, 1999.

———. *The Country Houses of Sir John Vanbrugh*. London: Aurum, 2009.

Nicholls, John. "The progresses . . . of King James the First." London, 1828.

Nicolson, Nigel. *Great Houses in Britain*. London: Weidenfeld and Nicolson, 1968.

Noble, Charles, and Alison Yarrington. "Like a Poet's Dreams." *Apollo* (26 October 2009): 46–53.

Obee, Hannah. "The Golden Age Returns." *Apollo* (26 May 2008): 60–66.

Pailthorpe, Richard, et al, eds. *Syon House*. Syon: Syon Park, 2003

Parissien, Steven. *Palladian Style*. London: Phaidon, 1994.

———. *Regency Style*. London: Phaidon, 1992.

Pembroke, Earl of. *Wilton House*. Wilton: Wilton House Trust, 1972.

Powers, Alan. *The Twentieth Century House in Britain*. London, Aurum: 2004.

Praz, Mario. *An Illustrated History of Interior Decoration from Pompeii to Art Nouveau*. London: Thames and Hudson, 1964 (reprinted 1982).

Ricketts, Annabel. *The English Country House Chapel: Building a Protestant Tradition*. London: Spire Books, 2007.

Ridgway, Christopher, and Nicholas Howard. *Castle Howard*. Castle Howard: Castle Howard Estate, 2008.

Robinson, John Martin. *Arundel Castle*. Chichester: Phillimore, 1994.

———. *The Dukes of Norfolk*. Chichester: Phillimore, 1995.

———. *The Last Country Houses*. London: Bodley Head, 1984.

———. *The Regency Country House*. London: Aurum, 2005.

———. *Wilton House*. Wilton: Wilton House Trust, 2010.

———. *The Wyatts: An Architectural Dynasty*. Oxford: Oxford University Press, 1979.

Robinson, John Martin, and Thomas Woodcock. *Heraldry in National Trust Houses*. London: The National Trust, 2001.

Rowan, Alistair. *Bob the Roman*, exhibition catalogue. London: Sir John Soane's Museum, 2003.

Sackville-West, Vita. *Berkeley Castle*. English Life Publications, 1972.

———. *English Country Houses*. London: Collins, 1942.

Saumarez-Smith, Charles. *The Building of Castle Howard*. London: Faber and Faber, 1990.

Schmidt, Leo. "Holkham Hall." *Country Life* (April 6, 2006): 106–11.

Schmidt, Leo, et al., ed. *Holkham Hall*. London and Munich: Prestel, 2005.

Schwartz, Selma, et al. *Waddesdon Companion Guide*, 3rd ed. Waddesdon: The National Trust at Waddeson, 2008.

Screech, Timon. "The Cargo of the New Year's Gift," Symposium in Memory of Dr. Oliver Impey, Ashmolean Museum, Oxford, May 31, 2006.

Sellars, Jane. *The Art of Thomas Chippendale*. Harewood: Harewood House Trust, 2000.

Smith, David. "Herbert, Philip, First Earl of Montgomery and Fourth Earl of Pembroke (1584–1650)." In *Oxford Dictionary of National Biography*, edited by H.C.G. Matthew and Brian Harrison, 714–18. Oxford and New York: Oxford University Press, 2004.

Snodin, Michael, ed. *Rococo: Art and Design in Hogarth's England*. London: Trefoil and the Victoria and Albert Museum, 1984.

Snodin, Michael, and Nigel Llewellyn, eds. *Baroque 1620–1800: Style in the Age of Magnificence*. London: V&A Publishing, 2009.

Spencer-Churchill, Lady Henrietta. *Classic English Interiors*. London: Collins and Brown, 2001.

———. *Classic Decorative Details*. London: Collins and Brown, 2003.

Stamp, Gavin. *Edwin Lutyens: Country Houses*. London: Aurum, 2001.

Steegman, John. *The Rule of Taste from George I to George IV*. London: Macmillan, 1936.

Stillman, Damie. *The Decorative Work of Robert Adam*. Albuquerque, N.M.: Transatlantic Arts, 1966.

Stone, Lawrence. "The Building of Hatfield House." In *Family and Fortune*, 62–91. Oxford: Oxford University Press, 1973.

Stroug, Roy. *Britannia Triumphans*. London: Thames and Hudson, 1981.

Strong, Roy, Marcus Binney and John Harris, eds. *The Destruction of the Country House, 1875–1974*. London: Thames and Hudson, 1974.

Summerson, John. *Architecture in Britain 1530–1830*, rev. ed. London: Penguin, 1983.

Summerson, John. *Inigo Jones*, 2nd rev. ed. New Haven and London: Yale University Press, 2000.

Tait, Alan. *Adam Brothers in Rome: Drawings from the Grand Tour*, exhibition catalogue. London: Sir John Soane's Museum, 2009.

Tatham, Charles, with engravings by Henry Moses. *The Gallery at Castle Howard*. 1811. Taylor, Stephen.

"Walpole, Robert (1676–1745)." In *Oxford Dictionary of National Biography*, edited by H.C.G. Matthew and Brian Harrison, vol. 57. Oxford and New York: Oxford University Press, 2004.

Thompson, Francis. *A History of Chatsworth*. London: Country Life, 1949.

Thornton, Peter. *Seventeenth Century Interior Decoration in England, France and Holland*. New Haven and London: Yale University Press, 1978.

Tritton, Veronica. *Parham and the Clive Pearsons*, bound offprint at Parham, originally published in *Antique Collector*, July 1987.

Turner, Jane. *The Dictionary of Art*. London: Macmillan, 1996.

Wainwright, Clive. *The Romantic Interior: The British Collector at Home, 1750–1850*. London and New Haven: Yale University Press, 1989.

Walpole, Horace, letter to George Montagu, 1 September 1760. In *The Letters of Horace Walpole*, vol. 3, edited by Peter Cunningham, 337. London: Richard Bentley and Sons, 1891.

Watkin, David. *The Classical Country House*. London: Aurum, 2010.

Wells-Cole, Anthony. *Art and Decoration in Elizabethan and Jacobean England: The Influence of Continental Prints 1558–1625*. London and New Haven: Yale University Press, 1997.

Wilson, Michael. *The English Country House and Its Furnishings*. London: Batsford, 1977.

Wilton, Andrew, ed. *Grand Tour: The Lure of Italy in the Eighteenth Century*. London: British Museum, 1997.

Wood, Martin. *John Fowler: Prince of Decorators*. London: Frances Lincoln, 2007.

———. *Nancy Lancaster: English Country House Style*. London: Frances Lincoln, 2005.

Woodcock, Thomas, and John Martin Robinson. *The Oxford Guide to Heraldry*. Oxford: Oxford University Press, 1988.

Worsley, Giles. *Inigo Jones and the European Classicist Tradition*. New Haven and London: Yale University Press, 2007.

NOTES

INTRODUCTION

1. Gore, *The History of English Interiors*; McQuorquodale, *The History of Interior Decoration*; Praz, *An Illustrated History of Interior Decoration*; Calloway, *The Elements of Style*; Girouard, *Life in the English Country House*; Garnett, *Living in Style*; Jackson, *The V&A Guide to Period Style*; Montgomery-Massingberd, *Great Houses of England and Wales*; Honour and Fleming, *Penguin Dictionary of the Decorative Arts*; Lancaster, *Here of All Places*.
2. McQuorquodale, *The History of Interior Decoration*, 9–27.
3. Gore, *The History of English Interiors*, 11–19.
4. McQuorquodale, *The History of Interior Decoration*, 81–84; also see Wells-Cole, *Art and Decoration in Elizabethan and Jacobean England*.
5. Musson, *Plasterwork*, 6–7, 12–23; Woodcock and Robinson, *Heraldry in National Trust Houses*, 7–22; Beard, *Craftsmen and Interior Decoration in England*.
6. Gore, *The History of English Interiors*, 41–44.
7. McQuorquodale, *The History of Interior Decoration*, 106.
8. Garnett, *Living in Style*, 86–88.
9. Gore, *The History of English Interiors*, 54.
10. McQuorquodale, *The History of Interior Decoration*, 102–04; Garnett, *Living in Style*, 94–95.
11. Garnett, *Living in Style*, 100–03; Summerson, *Architecture in Britain*, 319–419; Parissien, *Palladian Style*.
12. Campbell, *Vitruvius Britannicus*, 1.
13. Gore, *The History of English Interiors*, 68.
14. Musson, *Plasterwork*, 40–60; also see Beard, *Stucco and Decorative Plasterwork in Europe*.
15. Garnett, *Living in Style*, 24–25; Jackson-Stops, *The Treasure Houses of Britain*, 40–59 and 214–395; also see Wilton, *Grand Tour*.
16. Snodin, *Rococo*, 189–209; Chalcraft, *Strawberry Hill*.
17. Chippendale, *The Gentleman and Cabinet-Maker's Director*, 16.
18. Harris, *The Genius of Robert Adam*, 16; McQuorquodale, *The History of Interior Decoration*, 135–61.
19. Adam and Adam, *Works in Architecture*, 1.
20. Gore, *The History of English Interiors*, 103–04.
21. Robinson, *The Regency Country House*, 74–85.
22. Garnett, *Living in Style*, 152–58; Gore, *The History of English Interiors*, 123–31 and 142; see also Aldrich, *Gothic Revival*, and Wainwright, *The Romantic Interior*.
23. Stamp, *Edwin Lutyens*, 11–13, 140–49.
24. Hall, *The Victorian Country House*, 152–59; Harris, *Moving Rooms*, 59–68.
25. Garnett, *Living in Style*, 180–81; Powers, *The Twentieth Century House in Britain*, 54–57.
26. Strong, *The Destruction of the Country House*; Jackson-Stops, *The Treasure Houses of Britain*.
27. Garnett, *Living in Style*, 182–83; Gore, *The History of English Interiors*, 181–82; also see Cornforth, *Inspiration of the Past*, 158–81; Wood, *John Fowler*; and Wood, *Nancy Lancaster and Country House Style* (2005).

1 · HATFIELD HOUSE

1. *Hatfield Guidebook*; Croft, *Patronage*, 67–95; Stone, "The Building of Hatfield House"; Cecil, *The Cecils of Hatfield House*; Croft, "Cecil Robert," 746–59; and advice from Robin Harcourt Williams and the Marquis of Salisbury.
2. Nicholls, "The progresses … of King James the First," 129–31.
3. Croft, *Patronage*, 67, 80; Stone, "The Building of Hatfield House," 64, 79–80.
4. Stone, "The Building of Hatfield House," 32, 83.
5. Croft, *Patronage*, 68.
6. Ibid., 121.
7. Screech, "The Cargo of the New Year's Gift," 20.
8. Woodcock and Robinson, *The Oxford Guide to Heraldry*, 10–17.
9. Stone, "The Building of Hatfield House," 83; Croft, *Patronage*, 77.
10. Stone, "The Building of Hatfield House" 84; Croft, *Patronage*, 79.
11. Croft, *Patronage*, 84.
12. Ibid., 80–86.
13. Advice on original location of mosaic portrait from Robin Harcourt Williams
14. Stone, "The Building of Hatfield House," 84–85; Croft, *Patronage*, 85.

2 · WILTON HOUSE

1. Robinson, *Wilton House*; Cornforth and Hill, *Caroline*, 75–76; Bold, *Wilton House and English Palladianism*; Worsley, *Inigo Jones*; Earl of Pembroke, *Wilton House*; Summerson, *Inigo Jones*; Smith, "Herbert, Philip"; Watkin, *The Classical Country House*, 25–29; advice from John Martin Robinson, the Earl of Pembroke, and Chris Rolfe.
2. Robinson, *Wilton House*, 6–7.
3. Ibid., 6; Watkin, *The Classical Country House*, 25–26, 29.
4. Barbet, *Livre*.
5. Dick, *Aubrey's Brief Lives*, 225.
6. Robinson, *Wilton House*, 7.
7. Ibid., 5.
8. Duncan-Jones, *Sir Philip Sidney*,
9. Robinson, *Wilton House*, 24.
10. Cornforth and Hill, *Caroline*, 75–76.
11. Smith, "Herbert, Philip," 717–18.
12. Cornforth and Hill, *Caroline*, 75.
13. Cornforth and Hill, *Caroline*, 75.
14. Information from Chris Rolfe and Lord Pembroke.

3 · BOUGHTON HOUSE

1. Buccleuch, Lister, and Fitzpatrick, *Boughton*; Jackson-Stops, "French and Dutch Influence"; Cornforth, *Early Eighteenth Century Interiors*, 117–20; Metzer, "Montagu, Ralph, First Duke of Montagu"; Murdoch, *Boughton House*; Murdoch, *Noble Households*, 49–77; advice from the Duke of Buccleuch, Charles Lister, Gareth Fitzpatrick, Tessa Murdoch and John Hardy.
2. Murdoch, *Boughton House*, 20.
3. Ibid., 22
4. Ibid., 129.
5. Ibid., 58
6. Buccleuch, *Boughton*, 30.
7. Murdoch, *Boughton House*, 72.
8. Buccleuch, *Boughton*, 30.
9. Cornforth, *Early Eighteenth Century Interiors*, 116–18.
10. Murdoch, *Boughton House*, 72; Cornforth, *Early Eighteenth Century Interiors*, 84–85, 118–19.
11. Metzer, "Montagu, Ralph, First Duke of Montagu," 762.
12. Murdoch, *Boughton House*, 22.
13. Ibid., 28–30.

4 · CHATSWORTH

1. Fowler, *Chatsworth*; Thompson, *A History of Chatsworth*; Devonshire, *The House*; Lees-Milne, *English Country House: Baroque*; "William, Talman" in Colvin, *A Biographical Dictionary of British Architects*, 1007–14; Hosford, "Cavendish, William"; advice from Matthew Hirst, Hannah Obee, Charles Noble, the Duke and Duchess of Devonshire, Annabel Westman, David Mlinaric, Jonathan Bourne.
2. Thompson, *Chatsworth*, 34–48.
3. Musson, "Chatsworth, Derbyshire."
4. Observations made to the author by furniture expert John Hardy.
5. Hosford, "Cavendish, William."
6. Fowler, *Chatsworth*, 33.
7. Ibid., 26.
8. Ibid., 38–45.
9. Obee, "The Golden Age Returns," 65.
10. Morris, *The Illustrated Journeys of Celia Fiennes*, 106.
11. Walpole, letter to George Montagu.
12. Devonshire, *The House*, 131.
13. Annabel Ricketts, *The English Country House Chapel: Building a Protestant Tradition* (2007), 191–95.
14. Hosford, "Cavendish, William," 670.
15. Obee, "The Golden Age Returns," 60–66.

5 · CASTLE HOWARD

1. Ridgway and Howard, *Castle Howard*; Saumarez-Smith, *The Building of Castle Howard*, 89–115; Musson, *The Country Houses of Sir John Vanbrugh*, 30–67; Hart, *Sir John Vanbrugh*, 129–35; Lees-Milne: *English Country Houses: Baroque*, 148–165; advice from Dr. Christopher Ridgway and Simon Howard.

2. Hart, *Nicholas Hawksmoor*, 111–29.
3. Musson, *The Country Houses of Sir John Vanbrugh*, 21; Ridgway and Howard, *Castle Howard*, 12–15.
4. Musson, *The Country Houses of Sir John Vanbrugh*, 130–45.
5. Saumarez-Smith, *The Building of Castle Howard*, 94–104.
6. Saumarez-Smith, *The Building of Castle Howard*, 107–08; Ridgway and Howard, *Castle Howard*, 32–35.
7. Saumarez-Smith, *The Building of Castle Howard*, 105.
8. Ibid., 108.
9. Beard, *The Work of John Vanbrugh*, 36.
10. Saumarez-Smith, *The Building of Castle Howard*, 108.
11. Musson, *The Country Houses of Sir John Vanbrugh*, 106.
12. Saumarez-Smith, *The Building of Castle Howard*, 108–12.

6 · HOUGHTON HALL

1. Cornforth, *Houghton Hall*; Cornforth, *Early Eighteenth Century Interiors*, 134–88; Mowl, *William Kent*; Taylor, "Walpole, Robert"; "Kent, William (1685–1748)," in Colvin, *A Biographical Dictionary of National Biography*, 612–19; Murdoch, *Noble Households*, 169–205; advice from the Marquis of Cholmondley, John Morgan, and John Hardy.
2. "Kent, William (1685–1748)," in Colvin, *A Biographical Dictionary of National Biography*, 612–14.
3. Colvin, "Vardy, John," 1074–76.
4. Taylor, "Walpole, Robert, 67–92.
5. Ibid., 76.
6. Cornforth, *Early Eighteenth Century Interiors*, 154–55.
7. Ibid., 155–59; Cornforth, *Houghton Hall*, 34–39.
8. Cornforth, *Early Eighteenth Century Interiors*, 154–57.
9. Observation to the author from furniture expert John Hardy.
10. Cornforth, *Early Eighteenth Century Interiors*, 163–66.
11. Ibid., 164–65.
12. Significant items of Kent-designed furniture have been subject to acceptance in lieu arrangements and are vested in the Victoria and Albert Museum and displayed in their original context for the visiting public.

7 · HOLKHAM HALL

1. Hardy "The Interiors," 137–70; Leicester, *Holkham*; Cornforth, *Early Eighteenth Century Interiors*, 313–24; Hussey, *English Country Houses*, 131–46; Lees-Milne, *Earls of Creation*, 221–23; Colvin, "Kent, William," 612–19; "Brettingham, Matthew," in Colvin, *A Biographical Dictionary of British Architects*, 612–19; Murdoch, *Noble Households*, 207–30; Watkin, *The Classical Country House*, 53–58; advice from John Hardy, the Earl of Leicester, and Viscount Coke.

2. Schmidt, *Holkham Hall*, 97
3. Ibid., 30.
4. Ibid., 176; Leicester, *Holkham*, 16–19.
5. Schmidt, *Holkham Hall*, 100–03.
6. Ibid., 92.
7. Ibid., 101; Leicester, *Holkham*, 25–27.
8. Schmidt, *Holkham Hall*, 144–45; Leicester, *Holkham*, 32–35.
9. Schmidt, *Holkham Hall*, 144; for the furniture see Cornforth, *Early Eighteenth Century Interiors*, 213–14.
10. Schmidt, *Holkham Hall*, 144 (for Admiral Boscawen) and 164–70 for the statue gallery; also see Angelicoussis, *The Holkham Collection*.
11. Schmidt, *Holkham Hall*, 150–51; Cornforth, *Early Eighteenth Century Interiors*, 92–93.
12. Schmidt, *Holkham Hall*, 151.
13. Cornforth, *Early Eighteenth Century Interiors*, 313.
14. Schmidt, "Holkham Hall."

8 · HAREWOOD HOUSE

1. Harris, *The Genius of Robert Adam*, 132–55; Harris, *The Country Houses of Robert Adam*, 84–91; Stillman, *The Decorative Work of Robert Adam*; Harewood, *Harewood*; Sellars, *The Art of Thomas Chippendale*; and advice from Anna Robinson and John Hardy.
2. Harris, *The Genius of Robert Adam*, 133.
3. Ibid., 138.
4. Harewood, *Harewood*, 24–25; Sellars, *The Art of Thomas Chippendale*, 36.
5. Sellars, *The Art of Thomas Chippendale*, 34–35.
6. Ibid., 25–38.
7. Harris, *The Genius of Robert Adam*, 150–51.
8. Ibid., 139–41.
9. Sellars, *The Art of Thomas Chippendale*, 40–47; the restoration of the state bed was supported with a grant from the Heritage Lottery Fund.
10. Harris, *The Genius of Robert Adam*, 141–43.
11. Harewood, *Harewood*, 33–35.
12. Ibid., 44–45.
13. Harris, *The Genius of Robert Adam*, 149; Harewood, *Harewood*, 46–47.
14. Sellars, *The Art of Thomas Chippendale*, 22.

9 · SYON HOUSE

1. Pailthorpe, *Syon House*; Harris, *The Genius of Robert Adam*, 65–83; Harris, *The Country Houses of Robert Adam*, 54–65; Tait, *Adam Brothers in Rome*; Alistair Rowan, *Bob the Roman*; Stillman, *The Decorative Work of Robert Adam*; Adam and Adam, *Works in Architecture*; advice from Lisa Little and John Hardy.
2. Adam and Adam, *Works in Architecture*.
3. Ibid., 1–2
4. Ibid., 2.
5. Ibid., 2; Harris, *The Genius of Robert Adam*, 68–72.
6. Adam and Adam, *Works in Architecture*, 3; Harris, *The Genius of Robert Adam*, 69–70.
7. Harris, *The Genius of Robert Adam*, 72–74.
8. Adam and Adam, *Works in Architecture*, 3.
9. Harris, *The Country Houses of Robert Adam*, 59.
10. Adam and Adam, *Works in Architecture*, 3; Harris, *The Genius of Robert Adam*, 76–78; Pailthorpe, *Syon House*, 42.
11. Adam and Adam, *Works in Architecture*, 3.
12. Harris, *The Genius of Robert Adam*, 80–81.

10 · GOODWOOD HOUSE

1. Baird, *Goodwood*, 14–27, 84–93, 120–37, 146–55, 178–84; Baird, "The Refurbishment of the State Rooms at Goodwood House," 3–5; Baird, "Goodwood House," 44–51; Jacques, *A Visit to Goodwood*; Miller, *Hidden Treasure Houses*, 122–43; Robinson, *The Wyatts*; and advice from the Earl of March, James Peill, and Rosemary Baird.
2. Colvin, "Wyatt, James," 1175–89.
3. Jacques, *A Visit to Goodwood*, 18–27.
4. Baird, *Goodwood*, 180.
5. Jacques, *A Visit to Goodwood*, 27.
6. Ibid., 21.
7. Ibid., 66.
8. Baird, *Goodwood*, 150.
9. Ibid., 180.
10. Ibid., 197–209.

11 · REGENCY REINVENTION

1. Robinson, *The Regency Country House*; Cornforth, *English Interiors*; advice from John Martin Robinson.
2. Cornforth, *English Interiors*, 19.
3. Robinson, *Wilton House*, 10–11, 34–47.
4. Ibid., 11.
5. John Martin Robinson, *Arundel Castle*, 27–42.
6. Ibid., 34–35.
7. Cornforth, *English Interiors*, 40–41; Ridgway, *Castle Howard*, 50–53.
8. Tatham, *The Gallery at Castle Howard*; also see Cornforth, *English Interiors*, 41.
9. Fowler, *Chatsworth*, 54–65.
10. Devonshire, *The House*, 177.
11. Ibid., 173–76.
12. Ibid., 178.
13. Ibid., 179.
14. Ibid., 183; Noble and Yarrington, "Like a Poet's Dreams," 46–53.
15. Advice from Matthew Hirst.

12 · ARUNDEL CASTLE

1. Robinson, *Arundel Castle*; Robinson, *The Dukes of Norfolk*, 212–39; Miller, *Hidden Treasure Houses*, 12–33; Girouard, *The Victorian Country House*, 394; Hall, *The Victorian Country House*, 184–89; advice from John Martin Robinson and Sara Rodger.
2. Robinson, *The Dukes of Norfolk*, 214–24

3. Robinson, *Arundel Castle*, 54, 88; Hill, *God's Architect*.
4. Robinson, *Arundel Castle*, 42–60.
5. Ibid., 54.
6. Ibid., 54–55.
7. Ibid., 71–75.
8. Ibid., 66–69.
9. Robinson, *The Dukes of Norfolk*, 225.
10. Robinson, *Arundel Castle*, 69.

13 · WADDESDON MANOR

1. Schwartz, *Waddesdon Companion Guide*; Hall, *Waddesdon Manor*; Hall, *The Victorian Country House*, 152–61; Cornforth, "Waddesdon Manor"; de Rothschild, *The Rothschilds at Waddesdon Manor*; Ferguson, *The World's Banker*; Girouard, *The Victorian Country House*, 291–302; additional advice from Michael Hall, Pippa Shirley, and Diana Stone.
2. Hall, *Waddesdon Manor*, 100.
3. Ibid., 122–25; and Michael Hall, conversation with the author.
4. Hall, *Waddesdon Manor*, 125.
5. Ibid., 122.
6. Ibid., 73.
7. Ibid., 120; Schwartz, *Waddesdon Companion*, 19, 193.
8. Schwartz, *Waddesdon Companion*, 19, 193.
9. Hall, *Waddesdon Manor*, 105.
10. Schwartz, *Waddesdon Companion*, 61.
11. Cornforth "Waddesdon Manor," 122–27.
12. Hall, *Waddesdon Manor*, 221–24.

14 · BERKELEY CASTLE

1. Berkeley, *Berkeley Castle*; Sackville-West, *Berkeley Castle*; Miller, *Hidden Treasure Houses*, 36–55; Miller, "Berkeley Castle"; Hussey, "Berkeley Castle, Gloucestershire," 1430–33; Musson, *The English Manor House*; Aslet, *The Last Country Houses*, 182–256; Hartley, "Randal Thomas Mowbray Rawdon Berkeley," 167–82; Berkeley, *Beaded Bubbles*, 54–83, 92–105; Harris, *Moving Rooms*, 80–85; additional advice from Charles Berkeley and David Smith.
2. Cornforth, *The Inspiration of the Past*, 36–43.
3. Berkeley, *Berkeley Castle*, 2.
4. Miller, *Hidden Treasure Houses*, 36–55
5. Berkeley, *Beaded Bubbles*, 88.
6. Hartley, "Randall Thomas Mowbray Rawdon Berkeley," 176–77.
7. Ibid., and Miller, "Berkeley Castle," 74.
8. Miller, "Berkeley Castle," 57–59.
9. Ibid., and Harris, *Moving Rooms*, 84–85.
10. Cornforth, *Early Eighteenth Century Interiors*, 207.
11. Miller, "Berkeley Castle," 59.
12. Aslet, *The Last Country Houses*, 174–81.
13. Miller, "Berkeley Castle," 75.
14. Hartley, "Randall Thomas Mowbray Rawdon Berkeley," 180.

15 · PARHAM PARK

1. Girouard, *Life in the English Country House*, 308–18; Kirk, *Parham*; Tritton, *Parham and the Clive Pearsons*; *Parham Guidebook*; Cornforth, *The Inspiration of the Past*, 35–43; Cornforth, "Parham Park Revisited," 1566–70; 1658–62; and advice from Lady Emma Barnard, James Barnard, Richard Pailthorpe, and Lyndey Kessell.
2. Tritton, *Parham and the Pearsons*, 2.
3. Ibid., 2.
4. Musson *The English Manor House*, 20–21; Cornforth, *The Inspiration of the Past*, 20–46; Aslet, *The Last Country Houses*, 37–43.
5. Tritton, *Parham and the Pearsons*, 4.
6. Kirk, *Parham*, 157–58.
7. Musson, *English Manor House*, 108–115.
8. Kirk, *Parham*, 158–59.
9. Ibid., 87–89.
10. Ibid., 131–36; Tritton, *Parham and the Pearsons*, 7.
11. Tritton, *Parham and the Pearsons*, 3.

17 · LIVING INTERIORS

1. Strong, *The Destruction of the Country House*.
2. The. Hon Simon Howard, interview with the author, January 2011; information from Dr. Christopher Ridgway.
3. Gowers, *The Gowers Report on Outstanding Historical or Architectural Interest*.
4. Strong, *The Destruction of the Country House*, 11.
5. Jackson-Stops, *The Treasure Houses of Britain*.
6. Cornforth, *Inspiration of the Past*, 30–105, 106–07, 143–228; Wood, *John Fowler*, 280.
7. Wood, *Nancy Lancaster*.
8. Hughes, *John Fowler*.
9. Devonshire, "The Full Blown Country-House Look," 84.
10. David Mlinaric, interview with the author, January 2011.
11. Rosemary Baird, interview with the author, January 2011.
12. The Earl of March, interview with the author, January 2011.
13. Information from John Martin Robinson.
14. Mlinaric, interview.
15. The Earl of Pembroke, interview with the author, January 2011.
16. Ibid.
17. Advice from Robert Harcourt Williams, archivist at Hatfield; The Marquis of Salisbury, interview with the author, February 2011.
18. Information from Matthew Hirst and Hannah Obee of Chatsworth, 2010.
19. Ibid.
20. Mlinaric and Cecil, *Mlinaric On Decorating*, 152–71.
21. Mlinaric, interview with the author; also quoted in Massingberd, *Great Houses*, 142.